Battle Cry

*Reflections for Soul Readiness
and the Defense of the Gospel
in and out of Season*

James R. Fryer

While the past few decades have seen a growing fascination in the subject, much of it has lacked a truly biblical foundation. *Battle Cry*, however, is a breath of fresh air. Readers will find it thoroughly biblical, theologically sound, and extraordinarily practical. Drawing upon his years of missionary service in the Arctic, in Latin America as well as his service in the military chaplaincy, the author furnishes provocative, insightful questions at the end of each chapter. Pastors, church leaders and laymen will find it uniquely beneficial and eminently useful for classroom instruction, one-on-one discipleship, or personal study.

—Dr. Irv Busenitz, Professor *Emeritus* of Bible Exposition and Old Testament at the Master's Seminary.

Lashed to the cross, founded in the unshakeable Word of God both written and living, and flowing with personal experience, *Battle Cry* is a powerful reminder that we are one generation away at any given time from witnessing the abortion of Jesus' kingdom movement in a given locale if we do not stand and fight as men and women of God. We must battle for our marriages, our children, our churches, and our lost family members and friends, rejecting the world system while recognizing the reality of the daily spiritual conflicts and the weapons of our warfare which are mighty through God... Run to the battle and give your life for something worth dying!

—Dr. Chris Carr, Director, Global Gates Network Canada and Gateway Hub Leader for the Greater Toronto Area (globalgates.ca)

There are certain reminders in the Christian life which are always timely because they are timeless. The reminder, encouragement, admonishment regarding the spiritual battle the believer faces daily is a necessity. James Fryer has brought such a prompting in this book calling up history, recent and ancient, military practice, Christian hymnody, and biblical wisdom to illustrate the profound nature of the enemy's work in this world and the critical role that the believer must assume in the warfare. Essential then is the knowledge of the Word which *Battle Cry* appropriately advocates. There is no combat against the lies of the devil except through the Truth of God's Word. The challenge presented is to study and meditate upon the Word and prepare ourselves for the fight wielding the weapons made available to us through faith in Christ. Spiritual warfare is more about immersion in truth than it is about combating spiritual assailants. Praise the Lord for this encouraging book that reminds us of the power of the Word of God.

—John Evans, President of Good News Jail and Prison Ministry

Passionate, inspiring and challenging, *Battle Cry* calls the church and each individual believer to re-examine the subject of spiritual warfare. Thoroughly Biblical and creatively insightful, this work calls each Christian to be ready to defend their faith while positively engaging today's culture. Throughout the book, Fryer guides the reader through the disciplines and methods to equip the believer to carry out this task. Any Christian, especially those interested in missions, evangelism, apologetics, and pastoral ministries, will be greatly assisted by reading *Battle Cry*. I highly recommend this book.

—Dr. Robin Dale Hadaway, Professor of Missions, Midwestern Baptist Theological Seminary, Kansas City, Missouri.

Battle Cry by Dr. James R. Fryer

Dedicated to Sophia, Joshua, Jacob, Priscilla and Abraham

*Fight the good fight of the sacred gospel. Trust the
transformative power of our sovereign and holy Lord
through His Spirit and Word. Never forsake the battle
to live out the love of Christ in the fallen world around you.*

Acknowledgments

In the adversity of the Christian journey, I have been blessed, thus far, beyond measure with various mentors and models of what it means to take up the cross and follow Jesus Christ. I am grateful for the churches where myself along with my wife, Damaris and our children have had the privilege to serve and be nurtured by the community of Christ. As well, I am thankful for the faithful friends, pastors and professors that have served us in prayer and the formation of the Christian faith. Various helpers as well have blessed me in this project including those who have endorsed the book, and editors Ms. Wendy Chorot, Mr. Michael Conner and friends at Solid Ground Christian Books.

Table of Contents

Appendix A

Introduction

As a young husband, I recall challenging my wife of the reality of the spiritual war we face, that we must unequivocally be a people of the Word and "always being prepared to make a defense to anyone who asks you for a reason for the hope that is in you" (1 Peter 3:15). Now after being married for over 24 years—and being blessed with five children, seeing our first "baby" daughter finishing college, and son serving in the military—I recall a few months ago reminding my wife that we are in a spiritual war. The battle is unyielding, and it is unrelenting.

Throughout life, the opposition of spiritual darkness is continuous and merciless. The 3-fold axis of evil of the world, the flesh, and the devil continue to oppose the Holy Spirit and the perfect ways of God. Though we do not categorically blame everything on the being of Satan, we must see that the persistent ways the kingdom of darkness are intertwined with sin, death, and the seduction of worldliness, as the prince of the power of the air is persisting in his deception and lies.

This book is born out of my adversity, and the experience of the slow and difficult journey that I have been blessed to have experienced over the years. I was dramatically converted to Christ as a university student almost 30 years ago, and He has been ever faithful to me. The Lord has blessed me, led me, encouraged me, and watched over me through many "trials, toils and snares." I am sure this is only the beginning of the journey, but I have learned that moving in increments toward spiritual maturity and progressive sanctification is not a cakewalk; it is an arduous joy of discipline in a life often bent toward thinking in the flesh. Scripture tells us that it is all of grace to undeserving sinners.

Again, the battle is not easy, and it is not for the faint-hearted, the Apostle Paul exhorts the believer to be prepared in the Christian life as a warrior prepared for battle:

Finally, be strong in the Lord and in the strength of his might. Put on the whole armor of God, that you may be able to stand against the schemes of the devil. For we do not wrestle against flesh and blood, but against the rulers, against the authorities, against the cosmic powers over this present darkness, against the spiritual forces of evil in the heavenly places. Therefore take up the whole armor of God, that you may be able to withstand in the evil day, and having done all, to stand firm. Stand therefore, having fastened on the belt of truth, and having put on the breastplate of righteousness, and, as shoes for your feet, having put on the readiness given by the gospel of peace. In all circumstances take up the shield of faith, with which you can extinguish all the flaming darts of the evil one; and take the helmet of salvation, and the sword of the Spirit, which is the word of God, praying at all times in the Spirit, with all prayer and supplication. To that end, keep alert with all perseverance, making supplication for all the saints, and also for me, that words may be given to me in opening my mouth boldly to proclaim the mystery of the gospel, for which I am an ambassador in chains, that I may declare it boldly, as I ought to speak (Eph. 6:10-20).

The chapters of *Battle Cry* are organized into three parts. Firstly, part one—The Purpose, The Weapon, and Historical Reflection—consists of these three themes to set the tone that there is a purpose to the book, namely defending the "victorious" gospel. However, this foundational portion of *Battle Cry* also emphasizes that the weaponry God, our Defender and Refuge, has given to us is a holy gospel message that has already declared victory in the greatest battle. As well, two pieces that are brought out of great bodies of formative theological literature surround: 1) the period of the early church fathers; and 2) the era of the English and American Puritans.

Part two—Characteristics of the Cross-Centered Combatant—focuses on three roles of the Christian calling, explicitly, the

Christian as ambassador, soldier, and, fisherman. These are general traits that all Christians should aspire to. Certainly, such traits are associated with spiritual leadership, but in actuality they are the standard for all believers. Lastly, part three, titled Meditations for the Minefield of Life and Advancement of the Gospel, is the largest portion of the book. This section consists primarily of expositions of selected texts that are demonstrative of apologetic postures (gospel defensive "fighting positions") in the cross-centered life. The passages include traditionally considered apologetic texts like Jude 3: "Beloved, although I was very eager to write to you about our common salvation, I found it necessary to write appealing to you to contend for the faith that was once for all delivered to the saints." Part three also contains assorted topical studies in chapter 15 a topical study, focuses on waging spiritual combat for the well-being of your family, and chapter 16 on the cyclical nature of trials and tribulations that are a catalyst to our progressive sanctification. In the appendix, I have also included, a portion of *The Christian Soldier* by Puritan Thomas Watson.

In *Battle Cry*, I have aspired to appeal to modern-day pilgrims that no brother or sister in Christ would be deceived in the life and death battle that is raging, in our personal spheres, for our minds and souls. Oh, Christian, beware, the battle is fierce, and the enemy is a smooth-talking deceiver that accuses, destroys and devours. Let no one be deceived, there is a hellish opposition to all that is holy, and the alert Christian will not be subtly seduced. At the same time, we are called into the fray with a message from heaven. This is not only for seminary students, those gifted in evangelism, or ordained ministers. This is a call of every blood-bought follower of Jesus Christ.

For the ultimate preparedness, the gospel soldier must always be "training" for the inevitable attacks of the enemies of God, by being much in Scripture, "and in on His law he meditates day and night" (Ps. 1:2, NASB). Here the Christian may not rest upon his or her laurels, rather he or she is to stay fit for duty, disciplining his or her life for godliness, and aware of the schemes of the evil one. In his book *Demons: A Biblically Based Perspective*, Alex Konya writes:

> No matter how great the past victories or how blessed the spiritual experiences they may have enjoyed, believers must realize they are vulnerable to satanic or demonic shipwreck in their lives if they decide to cope in their own strength and refuse to walk in humble dependence upon God...Never in Scripture is the believer exhorted to seek out or attack the devil or his demons. On the contrary, the devil seeks to   attack the believer...The believer has been given his marching orders by God. He is to glorify God in his living and carry out the Great Commission. As he happily carries out these tasks, he will not need to be looking for Satan. Satan will be looking for him! So then, when   Satan attacks, the believer is to stand firm, being protected by the full armor of God.[1]

There is great comfort in these comments and points the believer back to the Word, where he or she is not instructed to wage an attack on the devil per se, but rather submit to omnipotent God (James 4:7), and to be busy with advancing the Great Commission until He comes. (Matt. 28: 18-20)

---

[1]Alex Konya, *Demons: A Biblically Based Perspective*, (Schaumburg: Regular Baptist Press, 1990), 102-103.

The Purpose, the Weapon, and Historical Reflection

Chapter 1

**The Battle Is Already Won:
The Stewardship of the
Victorious Gospel**

Consider momentarily how history has enjoyed decades of the alliance between the United States and the nation of Japan. Americans enjoy living in the culture and traveling to Japan, as Japanese have enjoyed living in the post WWII U.S. and traveling to the historical sight of Oahu, Hawaii, where the sneak attack on Pearl Harbor happened over 75 years ago. As WWII ended, a massive transition took place in the society of Japan. Due to the events of the war, particularly between the U.S. and Japan, Americans labeled August 14 as *Victory over Japan Day*, or *V-J Day*. The victory was announced by President Harry S. Truman in Washington that Japan had surrendered. The day was heralded as the very death of Fascist ideology.[2]

Though Fascism and the movement inspired by the deranged ideals upheld by Adolf Hitler were officially defeated, some time would pass as the Japanese culture would implement a new constitution and cultivate the more peaceable and capitalistic ideals in their society that exist today. Although the nation was freed from the agenda and views of Hitler, the vast majority of Japan still urgently needs the gospel. Henceforth, there was a transition period where

---

[2]History, V-J Day, World War II. http://www.history.com/topics/world-war-ii/v-j-day.

people began to turn away from the habits and views that had been embraced during the advancement of Communist-era thinking.

In a similar way, the Christian church worldwide has been given the stewardship of the gospel from the days of the apostles. As well, the significance and spiritual reality of the substitutionary sacrifice of Christ was declared in effect through the events of the crucifixion, resurrection and ascension of Jesus. Yet, the church continues to wrestle with and put away the unprofitable ways of the world, the flesh, and the devil. Turning aside from all forms of evil continues to be pursued.

From Ephesians 3:1-10, believers today should gain a powerful sense of confidence that the victorious gospel of Jesus Christ is profoundly in effect now, changing lives everywhere it is proclaimed and embraced. The stewardship of preserving, defending, and applying the gospel has been placed squarely upon the shoulders of the church from the days of the apostles unto today. The apostle Paul writes:

> For this reason, I, Paul, a prisoner for Christ Jesus on behalf of you Gentiles—assuming that you have heard of the stewardship of God's grace that was given to me for you, how the mystery was made known to me by revelation, as I have written briefly. When you read this, you can perceive my insight into the mystery of Christ, which was not made known to the sons of men in other generations as it has now been revealed to his holy apostles and prophets by the Spirit. This mystery is that the Gentiles are fellow heirs, members of the same body, and partakers of the promise in Christ Jesus through the gospel. Of this gospel I was made a minister according to the gift of God's grace, which was given me by the working of his power. To me, though I am the very least of all the saints, this grace was given, to preach to the Gentiles the unsearchable riches of Christ, and to bring to light for everyone what is the plan of the mystery hidden for ages in God who created all things, so that through the church the manifold

wisdom of God might now be made known to the rulers and authorities in the heavenly places (Eph. 3:1-10).

> Steward: A person who manages the property or financial affairs of another.

In looking at Ephesians 3:1-10, we see Paul's unique apostolic role of being a steward of the Word of God. You may also have, as I have, personally felt the awesome responsibility and privilege of being a caretaker of the vast spiritual treasure of the sacred gospel. Now, dozens of generations removed from the apostle Paul and the setting of the New Testament, along with untold millions around the world, I am a recipient of that gospel treasure and a modern-day steward of Scripture truth. Of course, Paul was a recipient of the divine revelation of the Bible (1 Peter 1:10-12; 2 Peter 1:20-21), as well as one to whom the revelation was entrusted to pass along to subsequent generations.

Every believer, since the preservation of the biblical corpus of all 66 books, is responsible for the stewardship of this very same Word. As Paul has spoken, "But even if we or an angel from heaven should preach to you a gospel contrary to the one we preached to you, let him be accursed. As we have said before, so now I say again: If anyone is preaching to you a gospel contrary to the one you received, let him be accursed" (Gal. 1:8-9).

A brief background on Paul as our spiritual progenitor, (one of the ancestors of the Christian faith that all believers may look back to): Paul was originally a blasphemer that persecuted the church of Jesus Christ (Gal. 1:11-14; 1 Tim. 1:13-14). In the early Christian church, Paul was one of the first church planting missionaries who transported and dispersed the message of Christ crucified. Your Bible may have a helpful map that depicts the church planting, gospel heralding excursions of the apostle Paul and his missionary teams.

Known as one of the four prison epistles (Ephesians, Colossians, Philippians, and Philemon), it is well-founded that Paul wrote

Ephesians while imprisoned in Rome. Chapter 3 verse 1 of Ephesians is seen as further evidence of this. There is strong evidence that though the letter was sent initially to Ephesus, it was also circulated throughout all of the churches of Asia Minor in the early church era. Paul's writing then in 3:1-10, while imprisoned for his faith, is expressing that he had been extraordinarily blessed to be a steward of the gospel.

At the time of the writing of his epistles, the message of the cross was being proclaimed and passed on to the Gentile nations (all non-Jewish people groups). Paul was not saying, nor does the New Testament say, that no Gentiles had heard. (Literally it was not that zero Gentiles had heard.) Rather, the situation was that in the age of the post-cross, gospel time period, he was given the responsibility to be a caretaker of the message of God, and that being primarily outside of the Jewish population to the Gentile peoples of the world. Thus in Ephesians 3:1, literally "Gentiles" meaning the "nations," the very same peoples referred to as "the uncircumcision" in 2:11. Paul was writing from Rome, where history tells us he eventually was beheaded for the gospel under a great wave of persecution by the Roman emperor Nero.

Every believer today, almost 2,000 years since Paul penned the letter to the Ephesians, is responsible for guarding the gospel message. All Christians are called to defend the message of God in a world of ungodly and at times hostile ideologies. However, Paul (along with other New Testament writers) had received the message and contents of his epistolary writings by the divine appointment of God. He had been granted the direct revelation of Holy Scripture and his role in the formation of the New Testament Canon.

Canon: The historically confirmed body of New Testament literature

---

So, Paul had a unique calling and role from God. This evermore emphasizes the grand design of God's international gospel program that was unfolding and that He had given Paul an extraordinary responsibility to fulfill (in bringing the gospel to the nations).

Ephesians 3:1-9 strikes me as highly profound to notice the way Paul spoke about the gospel and his own heart burden for the nations. It was compelling to consider his life transformation and that he was motivated to give his life for the progress of the gospel movement and for the personal benefit of the Ephesians. The wording of Ephesians 3:1-9 is remarkable; Paul uses phrases like: "stewardship of God's grace" (3:2); "insight into the mystery of Christ" (3:4); and "the administration of the mystery" (3:9, NASB). The imagery this brings to mind is of a wondrous heavenly management responsibility and calling from God. This should grip the New Testament believer firmly, helping him or her to grasp the intensity of Paul's burden.

Four observations of truth can be made—though more could be made—about the great responsibility of stewardship that the apostle Paul and others were burdened within the New Testament administration of the sacred gospel message. These four are: 1) the stewardship of the mystery of God revealed (Eph. 3:2-3); 2) the substance of the mystery of Christ (verses 4-6); 3) the grace of preaching (on the unfathomable riches of Christ) (verse 8); 4) the unveiling of the administration of the mystery (verse 9).

The English Baptist pastor, F.B. Meyer, affirms this grave responsibility that has been handed down through the ages of the mysteries of God in Christ. In his cherished devotional writings, he commented:

> We are God's trustees for men. To each of us is given some special phase of truth which we must pass on to others by the force of our character or by the teaching of our lips. It was given to Paul to make known the great truth that Gentiles might enter the Church of God on equal terms with Jews. During the earlier stages of human education this secret had

been withheld; but with the advent of the Son of man, the doors into the Church had been thrown open to all.[3]

The Stewardship of the Mystery of God Revealed

First off, Paul is found speaking of this "stewardship" of the grace of God, or "administration of God's grace" (Eph. 3:2-3, NIV). Paul is writing to the believers, initially in Ephesus, about how God had given him (Paul) the apostolic burden and responsibility for their behalf (to receive direct revelation from God and to bring or represent the message of God to them). The Gentiles—or peoples of the nations—were initially the main recipients of the writings of Paul. So, almost 2,000 years ago now, Paul wrote while imprisoned for this very gospel of the stewardship that is written of. He uses the figure of speech from οικονομιαν, literally of a "manager of a household," or of a business. It speaks of work, responsibility or arrangement of an administration (as of a house or property). In this administrative activity of an owner, Paul speaks of a *stewardship* (οικονομιαν) "for the fullness of time" (1:10), "the stewardship from God that is by faith" (1 Tim. 1:4); "the stewardship from God" (Col. 1:25).

Approximately 500 years ago, John Calvin wrote that this stewardship of God's grace is a "commission" from God.[4] In other words, God had commissioned Paul as one who is a manager of the divine message of the gospel. In a like manner we could say that since Paul was a receptor of the revelation of God, in that he received the inspired word from God, believers today are subsequently custodians and defenders of the canon of Scripture (the complete 66 books of the Old and New Testament). As well, believers should reflect on many ways they may consider themselves today to be stewards of the message of the gospel of God.

---

[3]F.B. Meyer- *A Devotional Commentary*, (public domain, 1914).

[4]John Calvin, *Commentaries on The Epistles of Paul to the Galatians and Ephesians*, (Grand Rapids: Baker Book House, 1998), 246-256.

The Substance of the Mystery of Christ

This section follows the former piece on the stewardship of the gospel mysteries. The apostle Paul describes that:

> When you read this, you can perceive my insight into the mystery of Christ, which was not made known to the sons of men in other generations as it has now been revealed to his holy apostles and prophets by the Spirit. This mystery is that the Gentiles are fellow heirs, members of the same body, and partakers of the promise in Christ Jesus through the gospel (Eph. 3:4-6).

Here he is explaining the profound implicational fullness for the nations. This insight, read by the early Christians in Ephesus, and to all who read it in subsequent generations, would have been glorious. This *insight* (συνεσιν) would have brought much clarity to their understanding, as if one gospel mystery (the inclusion of the Gentiles) was being unveiled within the unveiling of the larger gospel mystery of the whole Gentile and Jewish worlds together.

Paul clearly speaks of the truth he had received. Verse 5 clarifies, "which was not made known to the sons of men in other generations." Yet he goes on to say, "it has now been revealed ...This mystery is that the Gentiles [nations/peoples] are now fellow heirs, members of the same body." In another place, a related yet unique shade of this same mystery of Christ and His message revealed is Colossians 1:27: "To them God chose to make known how great among the Gentiles are the riches of the glory of this mystery, which is Christ in you, the hope of glory." Again, Paul uses the concept of the *mystery of Christ* to describe Christ in a   believer, the "hope of glory," yet overall in Ephesians 3:4-6 specifically that the Gentiles are wonderfully incorporated into this mystery.

This declaration would even have been surprising to the Jews of Paul's day til they had embraced the blessedness of the inclusion of the Gentiles into the "promise in Christ Jesus through the gospel"

14

(verse 6). Thus, saving faith in Jesus became the qualifier of being a genuine Israelite.

The Grace of Preaching

> Of this gospel I was made a minister according to the gift of God's grace, which was given me by the working of his power. To me, though I am the very least of all the saints, this grace was given, *to preach* to the Gentiles *the unsearchable riches of Christ* (Eph. 3:7-8, emphasis added).

Here is seen that it was the gift of God's grace that made Paul a minister and preacher of the message of Christ. Certainly, it is grace that Paul attributes for being made a gospel-servant. The word translated as *minister* is literally, a servant and generally refers to an attendant or table waiter. Here, the term reveals the New Testament connotation of a servant of the church, called by God to do the humble service of the ministry. This calling of God to be a servant of the gospel is as Paul says in Colossians 1:25, "according to the stewardship from God that was given to me for you, to make the word of God fully known." The service of ministry is characterized here with an aspect of tremendous humility.

Moving to Ephesians 3:8, Paul contrasts himself in a description of this extreme humility. He coins a term in Greek, translated "the *very least of all* saints" (τῷ ἐλαχιστοτέρῳ πάντων ἁγίων). The word actually means "the leaster" of all saints. Here he expresses the far less, far inferior sense. The humility of Paul is striking, never a false humility, but an actual assessment of himself. Similarly, in 1Timothy 1:15, Paul says he is the foremost of all sinners. Paul seemed well familiar and overwhelmed by this sense of unworthiness apart from the work of Christ (1 Cor. 15:9). Charles Hodge well expresses that:

Less than the least, ἐλαχιστοτέρος, a comparative formed from a superlative. It was not merely the sense of his sinfullness in general, which weighed so heavily on the apostle's conscience. It was the sin of persecuting Christ, which he could never forgive himself. As soon as God revealed his Son in him, and he apprehended the infinite excellence and love of Christ, the sin of rejecting and blaspheming such a Savior appeared so great that all other sins seemed as comparatively nothing.[5]

Again, Paul emphatically contrasts his lowly position with the magnificent responsibility of bearing the sacred message. He saw this as highly significant. The believer then as a student of the apostolic writings should see that this "stewardship" or management of the gospel message is to preach it to the nations. The word *preach* in Ephesians 3:8 (εὐαγγελίσασθαι) is literally, to announce the good news, or proclaim the gospel, to gospelize. This to proclaim the divine message of salvation; it is to bring someone into the relation of the message, to evangelize them. Paul writes that it was the grace of God that bestowed upon him this great stewardship of preaching. We could say here that this grace to preach was given to convey to the nations the riches of Christ (3:8). Yet, there are clearly other intended purposes.

The Jews at the time of the New Testament history would have understood this preaching to the nations if they were aware of their Old Testament writings. There is much in the Old Testament clarifying that the message was intended by God to be communicated freely to the nations (e.g., Ps. 67; Is. 49:6). This is something that the Lord Jesus taught as well (John 10:16). So, the direct clear teaching of the revealed doctrine of the incarnation or atoning sacrifice of Christ was not yet fully understood at the time.

---

[5]Charles Hodge, *A Commentary on the Epistle to the Ephesians,* (New York: Robert Carter and Bros., 1860), 1.8.

The mystery of Christ was not communicated fully in other generations, yet Paul communicates emphatically that the nations (Gentile people groups) are fellow heirs, fellow members, and fellow partakers. The fullness of times had brought this out in Paul's day and today the blessed and blood-bought body of Christ (His church) has the designated responsibility to tell the message of God. As well, this glorious understanding would have been surprising to much of the Jewish culture. Pastor/teacher John MacArthur states, "The idea of including the Gentiles in one body with Jesus was the spiritual equivalent of saying lepers were no longer to be isolated, that they were now free to intermingle and associate with everyone."[6]

Today, all Christians as gospel caretakers bear the mandate of the Great Commission (Matt. 28:19-20). The body of Christ today contains no apostles, in the same sense of those from the early days of the church, those who were with Jesus and received the revelation of the New Testament writings. The church today consists of those who absolutely sense this responsibility of being the protectors and defenders of the gospel, and who must tell the message to this modern age and pass it on to our children's children. In an ongoing application then, the stewardship of the mystery of the gospel of Jesus Christ continues until the Lord returns.

The Unveiling of the Administration of the Mystery

This unveiling—of the administration of the mystery of Christ—is tied here to the verses prior that speak of the grace given to Paul to preach the same mystery. Ephesians 3:9-10 follow, "and to bring to light for everyone what is the plan of the mystery hidden for ages in God, who created all things, so that through the church the manifold wisdom of God might now be made known to the rulers and authorities in the heavenly places." This charge then was passed

---

[6]John MacArthur, *The MacArthur New Testament Commentary: Ephesians,* (Chicago: The Moody Bible Institute, 1986), 91-92.

along by Paul and the apostolic age. It was a charge to be received by all subsequent generations and intended that all would be responsible for until the return of Christ. This is the inheritance of the commission given by Christ, first to the apostles and early disciples then to all successive generations.

The churches today as mentioned are the current caretakers of the gospel, to assure it is not distorted, misrepresented, or compromised. The saints of light in our modern era are the heirs of the treasure of the gospel. All Christians from the apostolic age onward have been commissioned not only to possess the gospel, but to obey, defend, and to publicize it geographically both near and far (Matt. 24:14; 28:19-20; John 14:23; James 1:22; 1 John 2:17).

Looking more succinctly at Ephesians 3:10, the making known of the "manifold wisdom of God" was to progress through the church unto the "rulers and authorities in the heavenly places." Certainly, this component of the declaration of the gospel began from the days of the apostles, but continues increasingly until this very day almost 2,000 years later. This is as much a part of the battle cry of victory today for the church as it was when Christ initially declared that the victory over sin and death was completed through His crucifixion, resurrection, and ascension.

As well, this battle cry continues to be sounded as the Kingdom of Jesus today advances in the penetration of spiritual darkness with the marvelous light of the gospel. There is then a modern sense that the message of Christ crucified continues to testify of the spiritual victory won at the cross. This victory is over many aspects of the ramifications of the curse upon man and creation. This includes a victory declared over all the effects of our fallenness (Eph. 2:1). It would encompass all moral and ethical corruption that stems from the effects on the mind, and reasoning of mankind (Jer. 17:9; Titus 3:3; 1 John 3:14; 5:12). Solomon, king of Israel, bore witness to the reality of the inner inability of man to live righteously in Ecclesiastes 9:3, "The hearts of the children of man are full of evil, and madness is in their hearts while they live, and after that they go to the dead."

18

God has made known His wisdom that is manifest in Scripture through His church and will continue to make His wisdom known through the ongoing stewardship of the gospel. Some Bible commentators hold that this is a witness of the church before the angelic hosts. For example, Calvin attested that this was a testimony before the holy angels of God in heaven:

> Paul's meaning is this: The church, composed both of Jews and Gentiles, is a mirror, in which angels behold the astonishing wisdom of God displayed in a manner unknown to them before. They see a work which is new to them, and the reason of which was hid in God. In this manner, and not by learning anything from the lips of men, do they make progress.[7]

Others observe from the text in Ephesians that the phrase about "rulers" and "authorities" is found almost identically in Eph. 3:10 to reference the holy angels, and 6:12, three chapters later to refer to the fallen and unholy demonic hosts. This lends to the view that both good and evil angels are being referred to here. Pastor/teacher John MacArthur in his commentary on Ephesians writes, "God has brought the church into being for the purpose of manifesting His great wisdom before the angels, both holy and unholy..."[8] It is certain that even the unholy angels are used in the unfolding of the sovereign purposes of God over the universe.

In concluding this section and the chapter, there is remarkable imagery to consider, that being the angels throughout heaven, and potentially the condemned demonic hosts of angels as well, that will bear witness by the life of the church. These angelic beings must bear witness of this great "administration" of the heavenly mystery in action in the world today. As eternity rolls onward, this glorious

---

[7]Calvin, *Ephesians*, 255-256.
[8]MacArthur, *Ephesians*, 96.

theme will resound always throughout the halls of the eternal heavenly Kingdom and will echo forth the righteous judgment of God in hell both in the demonic hosts and in the consciences of the damned (Dan. 12:2; Jude 7; Rev. 14:11).

Questions for Spiritual Formation:

1. What unique stewardship responsibilities did God give the apostle Paul to include the unique apostolic stewardship that all of the apostles were given?

2. As a Christian today what specific stewardship responsibilities has God given to you?

3. Why is the gospel like an amazing treasure of unlimited value to be protected and proclaimed?

4. Consider the sentence "angelic beings must bear witness of this great 'administration' of the heavenly mystery in action in the world today." What encouragement may this bring to the believer's heart that the mystery of the glorious gospel has been declared and all of heaven and its hosts/angelic creatures, and the demonic hosts of hell all testify to its reality?

Alas! and did my Savior bleed
by Isaac Watts

Alas! and did my Savior bleed
And did my Sov'reign die?
Would He devote that sacred head
For such a worm as I?

Was it for crimes that I had done
He groaned upon the tree?
Amazing pity! grace unknown!
And love beyond degree!

Well might the sun in darkness hide
And shut his glories in,
When Christ, the mighty Maker died,
For man the creature's sin.

Thus might I hide my blushing face
While His dear cross appears,
Dissolve my heart in thankfulness,
And melt my eyes to tears.

But drops of grief can ne'er repay
The debt of love I owe:
Here, Lord, I give myself away,
'Tis all that I can do.[9]

---

[9]Isaac Watts, Alas! And Did My Savior Bleed, (Public Domain, 1707).

Chapter 2   **The Sword of the Spirit:**
                                   The Word of God

General George Marshall (a paragon of principled officer-ship, referred to by Winston Churchill as 'that noble Roman') spoke of the 'beast within' which emerges inside the individual in combat. During World War II, Marshall was more concerned about controlling this beast to preserve good order and discipline within the ranks. However, in the information age, when this beast takes control, an insurgent may appear within our ranks who is far more politically dangerous than any insurgent we confront with arms on the battlefield—the moral insurgent.

To defeat this most dangerous insurgent, our Army's operational culture must learn that right conduct on the battlefield now matters more than anything else that we do. Good conduct cannot in itself win the peace, which often depends upon strategic conditions we soldiers do not control. But sound battlefield conduct, when combined with the right objectives and tactics, does marginalize insurgents by depriving them of the popular support that they need to thrive. Thus, as surreal as it sometimes seems to those of us who served in the 1990s, battlefield technology, armored vehicles, gunneries, and weapons ranges contribute less to our mission success today than does the ethical behavior of our troops.[10]

---

[10]http://usacac.army.mil/CAC2/MilitaryReview/Archives/English/Milita ryReview_20110930PofA_art017.pdf.

Just as the ethical conduct of the warrior may greatly determine the "mission success" on the field of battle, so it is the skilled holy character of the man of God that will prepare him for a godly effort in each spiritual battle that he will encounter. It is the skillful usage of the weapon of the Word, the Sword of the Spirit, that is the advantageous agent of change that can form the saint for the work of spiritual combat.

All Scripture is breathed out by God and profitable for teaching, for reproof, for correction, and for training in righteousness, that the man of God may be complete, equipped for every good work (2 Tim. 3:16-17).

The gospel soldier must have absolute confidence in the weapon issued to him. His spiritual weaponry, the Bible, must have a place of the utmost trust and underlying confidence in the heart of the believer. Without this confidence in the living Word given by our Maker, how can one have complete trust and confidence in the living God whose bountiful attributes are not only displayed in the general revelation of all creation, but also on every page of the inspired and written Word?

The Bible then is the spiritual fitness manual for the gospel worker, for the soldier of the cross. 2 Tim. 3:16-17 can be considered in two parts:

1) The Qualities of Scriptural Benefit
2) The Preparedness of the Man of God, the Formation of the Gospel Soldier.

The Qualities of Scriptural Benefit

The diligent Reformation leader, John Calvin, reflects profoundly in his Institutes (Book 1.6.3) about the essential nature of

Holy Scripture as the divinely given resource mercifully supplied to us by God to help us to know Him:

> For if we reflect how prone the human mind is to lapse into forgetfulness of God, how readily inclined to every kind of error, how bent every now and then on devising new and fictitious religions, it will be easy to understand how necessary it was to make such a depository of doctrine as would secure it from either perishing by the neglect, vanishing away amid the errors, or being corrupted by the presumptuous audacity of men.

> It being thus manifest that God, foreseeing the inefficiency of his image imprinted on the fair form of the universe, has given the assistance of his Word to all whom he has ever been pleased to instruct effectually, we, too, must pursue this straight path, if we aspire in earnest to a genuine contemplation of God - we must go, I say, to the Word, where the character of God, drawn from his works is described accurately and to the life; these works being estimated, not by our depraved judgment, but by the standard of eternal truth.[11]

Regarding these qualities mentioned of *Scriptural Benefit,* much could be written. What will be emphasized here is that by its own definition, the Bible is "God breathed" (θεοπνευστος), it is breathed or aspirated forth from heaven, and it has certain qualities or functions for which God intended it. The phrasing here tells us that the Bible is inspired by God, as no other writing has been. The understanding of the early believers is that both the Old Testament— that told of creation or the beginning of history, the curse that fell upon the world due to the cause of sin, and the Savior/Messiah to

---

[11]John Calvin, *Institutes of the Christian Religion 1,* (Lousiville: Westminster John Knox Press, 1960), 6. 3.

come—as well as the entire New Testament—which contains the life and teachings of Jesus Christ, and the subsequent implications of the earth to date of the gospel message and the Kingdom of God—are given from God. All of both the Old Testament and New Testament are to be considered God-breathed or divinely inspired Scripture spoken forth from God Almighty.

It may be contemplated, *what is uniquely amazing about the Bible as divine communication?* Part of the treasure of the Bible is that just as the Creator has created and breathed life into man, so He has breathed forth a living Word and has established it as completely sufficient for all that human beings need, both to know God their Creator and to have the spiritual instruction needed to move through life as a wise man who knows well where he is going (not like a blind man wandering through the dark). In verse 16 of 2 Timothy 3, one reads that the Scriptures are profitable (this means helpful or advantageous) for the spiritual work of teaching, reproof (or rebuke), correction, for training in righteous (or training in godliness).

The reflective reader may ask: 1) "How are the God-breathed writings advantageous for spiritual teaching?"; 2) "How is the God-inspired Book helpful for reproof (or rebuking someone in sin)?"; 3) "How are the Scriptures most helpful for correction?"; and 4) "How is the Holy Bible most beneficial for training a Christian man or woman in righteousness or godliness?" These questions are considered in the remarks on the next few pages.

How are the God-breathed writings advantageous for spiritual teaching?

Regarding "teaching," the Book of God is most advantageous for the Christian because God has created us to be learners. All of what belongs to God that He has wanted to explain to His children is contained in the pages of the Bible. This very content of Scripture is that which the Divine Author wants us to know. The apostle Paul wrote these words originally to Timothy, an early church leader. Paul, along with Timothy, shows the church what a spiritual mentor relationship looks like.

Remarkably, Paul was teaching, training, and modeling Christian leadership for Timothy almost 2,000 years ago. As well, the Old Testament psalms echo back the same sentiment from 1,500 years before the apostle Paul wrote his epistle to Timothy. Psalm 119:33-34 expresses, "Teach me, O LORD, the way of your statutes; and I will keep it to the end. Give me understanding, that I may keep your law and observe it with my whole heart." This should also be the prayer of every Christian.

How is the God-inspired Book helpful for reproof?

Holy Scripture is help from heaven in the area of *reproof* (or rebuke). This means convicting or exposing sin and all unethical conduct. This is related to the growing awareness of such sinful, immoral, and unethical behavior or actions that one may need to confess in prayer to God. The Christian is himself or herself responsible before God to pursue spiritual growth and to cultivate a healthy and sensitive conscience. The wisdom literature is replete with such passages that bring reproof to the foolishness that the human heart is often enticed. Solomon writes:

Wisdom cries aloud in the street, in the markets she raises her voice; at the head of the noisy streets she cries out; at the entrance of the city gates she speaks: "How long, O simple ones, will you love being simple? How long will scoffers delight in their scoffing and fools hate knowledge? If you turn at my *reproof*, behold, I will pour out my spirit to you; I will make my words known to you. Because I have called and you refused to listen, have stretched out my hand and no one has heeded, because you have ignored all my counsel and would have none of my *reproof*, I also will laugh at your calamity; I will mock when terror strikes you, when terror strikes you like a storm and your calamity comes like a whirlwind, when distress and anguish come upon you" (Prov. 1:20-27, emphasis added).

Yet again, the ball is in the hands of the Christian to obey and heed the warning that Scripture beckons with.

How are the Scriptures most helpful for correction?

The God-breathed Scriptures are most beneficial for *correction* also; this is as well gained in 2 Timothy 3:16. The correction the Bible tells of is a setting something right again, the wording talks about restoring something to its original position that had fallen. It means helping someone back on their feet after they have stumbled. People have said, The Holy Spirit is a gentleman, it is true He is always ready with a helping hand to encourage and comfort someone, who has fallen down, back up upon their feet again (not negating His other roles like convicting, and teaching). The psalmist also writes, "Before I was afflicted I went astray, but now I keep your word" (Ps.119:67).

How is the Holy Bible most beneficial for training a Christian man or woman in righteousness or godliness?

Lastly is that the God-breathed Bible is very much heaven-sent aid for "*training in righteousness*" or godliness. This was originally used to describe the training of children and reflects that basic Christian upbringing. However, here it tells of church members, believers, growing under the guidance of the Word of God and being focused more on spiritual education. Of all the applications Paul gives, the saint should sense great assistance from God for the countless needs he or she faces in the Christian life. English Pastor F.B. Meyer, in his devotional writings, has said:

> In the stern experiences of human life there is no stay that is comparable to the Holy Scriptures. The infinite variety of

27

Scripture adapts itself to different states of the soul. Whatever our need, we can find its solace and remedy here. Thus we may live a complete life, finding in the Bible an equipment for all our emergencies. In this armory is every weapon for offense and defense; in this pharmacopoeia is a medicine and antidote for every wound.[12]

The Preparedness of the Man of God, the Formation of the Gospel Soldier

Again, the gospel worker must have absolute confidence in the God-breathed Scripture (γραφη θεοπνευστος). This is fundamental to the work. In the field of medicine, a cardiologist must have total trust that his or her training, knowledge, method, and expertise are adequate for the prognosis, preparation, cardiac surgery, and recovery plan. The cardiologists and cardiac surgeons at the nationally renowned cardiovascular institute at Johns Hopkins Hospital have been recognized for an entire generation for their skill. Their web site (www.hopskinsmedecine.org) explains that they have pioneered in both treatment and research in almost every field "related to cardiovascular disorders, from transplant surgery to prevention." By God's grace and His blessing on the development of medical care, this level of precision has granted the cardiologists at Johns Hopkins to be highly adequate and equipped for their particular challenges. The Scriptures received by the revelation of the Holy Spirit clearly express proficient enabling for the man of God (3:17).

The great purpose of the God-inspired Book for the believer is that the man of God (and all Christians) may be totally equipped for every good deed in life. This verse turns to the purpose statement, namely, "*that* the man of God may be complete, equipped for every good work" (emphasis added). Other modern translations use the phrase *so that...* This common Greek conjunction (ινα) is often used as a purpose clause conjunction (Mark 1:38; John 1:22; 3:15; 17:1)

---

[12]F.B. Meyer, *Through the Bible Day by Day* (Public Domain, 1914).

[13] and teaches the Christ-follower that the heaven-inspired Book is to be used in his or her own life (as seen in the comments for teaching, reproof, correcting, and training). The end purpose and result of making the "man of God" to "be complete, equipped for every good work" in life is so that he or she may do the "good work" given from God (Eph 2:10). In all that the Christian needs, he or she has gained in his or her spiritual life (through the Word and Spirit) to do what is necessary for the work. Thus, he or she is fully prepared or supplied for the task.

A description found in a related passage in Ephesians 4:12 tells of the equipping of the saints "for the work of ministry, for building up of the body of Christ." Furthermore, the idea is that the believer is adept, capable of whatever God puts before them because of this more than adequate training and equipping. He or she ought to be highly confident in life because the Lord has both prepared and equipped them well. As in military training for battlefield preparedness, so the making complete and the equipping of the "man of God" to be prepared fully for every good work is the noble goal of the gospel soldier.

One Christian leader who faithfully served Christ and lived out the teaching brought forth in this study is Dr. Wayne Mack. Mack's writing in the collection of articles in the volume "Totally Sufficient" asserts that:

> Believers have in Christ everything they will ever
> need to meet any trial, any craving, and any difficulty
> they might ever encounter in this life. Even the new-
> est convert possesses sufficient resources for every
> spiritual need ...There is nothing more—no great

---

[13]Henry Alford, The Greek Testament (Public Domain, 1873), "result of the profitableness of Scripture: reasons why God has, having Himself inspired it, endowed it with this profitableness."

transcendental secret, not ecstatic experience, no hidden spiritual wisdom—that Christians can take to some to higher plane of the spiritual life.[14]

Christians absolutely have not only the answers—and must not feel the necessity to search aimlessly outside of the truth of God—but also the precisely appropriate weaponry for the battles of life. Below are reflections about the sufficiency of the Scriptures to mature, help, sanctify, gratify, and heal in our lives. Seeing that all of Psalm 119 is a testimony of the glory of God, an ode to the Holy Scriptures as a whole, consider these twenty meditations from the 176 verses of Psalm 119, and the subsequent illustrations that serve as examples of such Bible sufficiency:

1) The Scriptures are permanently established by God in heaven and earth (verses 89-90).
2) The Scriptures are our counselors (verse 24).
3) The Scriptures, through mediation upon them, cultivate blessedness in the life of the saint (verses 1-2).
4) The Scriptures are the source of authentic joy in times of sorrow (verse 28).
5) The Scriptures are that which inspire reverence for the Lord (verse 38).
6) The Scriptures are the source of true revival (verses 25, 37, and 40).
7) The Scriptures produce in the believer a heart of freedom described as at liberty and openly (verse 45).
8) The Scriptures produce comfort in affliction (verses 50 and 76).
9) The Scriptures form within the Christian an attitude of thankfulness (verse 62).

---

[14]Ed Hindson and Howard Eyrich, *Totally Sufficient* (Eugene, Oregon: Harvest House Publishers, 1997), 28.

10) The Scriptures cultivate an attitude of appreciation through trials (verses 71, 75, and 92).
11) The Scriptures correct unbiblical perspectives concerning material things (verses 72 and 127).
12) The Scriptures guide us to walk in truth (verses 78 and 128).
13) The Scriptures produce in us perseverance (verses 83 and 87).
14) The Scriptures encourage us in trials (verse 92).
15) The Scriptures develop within us wisdom sufficient for our situations (verses 98-100).
16) The Scriptures illuminate our understanding (verses 105 and 130).
17) The Scriptures are the believer's source of help in danger (verses 109-110, and 117).
18) The Scriptures continually uphold an example of something refined and pure (like purified gold) (verse 140).
19) The Scriptures are the source of spiritual satisfaction (verses 148 and 162).
20) The Scriptures express the mercy of the Lord (verses 41, 149, and 159).

It is imperative then that believers trust in the sufficiency of the Bible. The Scriptures ought to be our model of help and we need to avoid using a mixture of biblical principles and concepts with unbiblical presuppositions and ideologies. In addition, let us consider another passage in our conclusion of this portion:

Everyone then who hears these words of mine and does them will be like a wise man who built his house on the rock. And the rain fell, and the floods came, and the winds blew and beat on that house, but it did not fall, because it had been founded on the rock. And everyone who hears these words of mine and does not do them will be like a foolish man who built his house on the sand. And the rain fell, and the floods came, and the winds blew and beat against that house, and it fell, and great was the fall of it" (Matt. 7:24-27).

The sufficiency of Scripture is the watershed issue of both true biblical counseling and all forms of biblical discipleship, if we are to succeed in cultivating a biblical outcome by the application of spiritual truth to the dilemmas and adverse situations of life and faith. There is no other option than to uphold the consistent philosophy that the Word of God is able to penetrate through all issues in the journey of sanctification to include the "deeper problems" of the human mind. From what may be seen as issues in spiritual warfare, the seemingly insurmountable obstacles of life's great circumstances must drive the saint to the Scripture where "the prophetic word more fully confirmed" can guide more effectively (2 Peter 1:19).

In his helpful book *Fighting Satan: Knowing His Weaknesses, Strategies, and Defeat*, Dr. Joel Beeke, president of Puritan Reformed Theological Seminary, writes about a biblical offense against the dark schemes of the devil. He includes:

> Intimately-acquaint yourself with the Bible by studying it and memorizing it daily. That will help keep God's sharp sword in your hand. Keep the sword polished and bright by living the Bible's truths each day. Keep the sword ready at all times through constant prayer. Speak out: bear witness to Scripture truth. Carry the light of God's Word into a dark world, shining its light into every dark corner.[15]

---

[15]Joel Beeke, *Fighting Satan: Knowing His Weaknesses, Strategies, and Defeat*, (Grand Rapids: Reformation Heritage Books, 2015), 53.

Questions for Spiritual Formation:

1. How are the God-breathed writings advantageous for spiritual teaching?

2. How is the God-inspired Book helpful for reproof (or rebuking someone in sin)?

3. How are the Scriptures most helpful for correction?

4. How is the Holy Bible most beneficial for training a Christian man or woman in righteousness or godliness?

5. Why is the sufficiency of Scripture the watershed issue of both true biblical counseling and all forms of biblical discipleship?

O' Blessed Bible
by Fanny Crosby

O blessed, blessed Bible,
Our treasured book divine,
With hope, and joy, and comfort,
Thy pages brightly shine.

Our chart upon life's ocean,
Our compass day by day,
The lamp our feet directing,
The light that guides our way.

Thou tellest us of Jesus,
The Son of God above,
Who came the world to ransom,
So great His wondrous love.

O blessed, blessed Bible,
That God himself hath giv'n,
To fit us for His kingdom,
Of endless life in Heav'n.

Chorus:

More precious still than rubies,
More pure than purest gold,
Our blessed, blessed Bible,
Thy worth can never be told.[16]

---

[16] Fanny Crosby, *O Blessed Bible* (Public Domain, 1895).

Chapter 3

Our Divine Defense:
The Source of Our Strength

The LORD is my rock and my fortress and my deliverer, my God, my rock, in whom I take refuge, my shield, and the horn of my salvation, my stronghold (Ps. 18:2).

Martin Luther, the great Reformer, wrote about 36 hymns in addition to his many books. Undoubtedly, the best known, A Mighty Fortress is Our God, magnifies the sovereign power and majesty of God. It is widely recognized that the song gained prominence early on as representative of the Protestant Reformation:

> It was sung at Augsburg during the Diet, and in all the churches of Saxony, often against the protest of the priest. It was sung in the streets; and, so heard, comforted the hearts of Melanchthon, Jonas, and Cruciger, as they entered Weimar, when banished from Wittenberg in 1547. It was sung by poor Protestant emigrants on their way into exile, and by martyrs at their death. It is woven into the web of the history of Reformation times, and it became the true national hymn of Protestant Germany.

> The hymn became closely associated with Luther himself, as it embodied in its words and melody so much of the character of its author — bold, confident, defiant in the face of opposition. association is symbolized in the monument to Luther at Wittenberg where the first line of the lyrics was engraved on the base. There are at least 7 documented theories on the

time and circumstances in which the hymn was written. Benson concludes, along with several other historians, that the most likely story is that it was written in October 1527 as the plague was approaching. The evidence for this date is the printing history surrounding it (no copies beforehand, and a growing number of copies afterward).

There is debate about where the tune came from. In times past, it was believed to have been borrowed by Luther, perhaps from an old Gregorian melody. More recently, however, scholars are inclined to believe that Luther wrote it himself. (The story that the tune came from a tavern song that was popular in Luther's day is the result of a misunderstanding of German musical terminology.)[17]

A Mighty Fortress Is Our God
by Martin Luther

A mighty fortress is our God,
a bulwark never failing;
our helper he amid the flood
of mortal ills prevailing.
For still our ancient foe
doth seek to work us woe;
his craft and power are great,
and armed with cruel hate,
on earth is not his equal.

Did we in our own strength confide,
our striving would be losing,
were not the right man on our side,
the man of God's own choosing.

---

[17]Tim Challies, "Hymn Stories, A Mighty Fortress is Our God," http://www.challies.com/articles/hymn-stories-a-mighty-fortress-is-our-god.

Dost ask who that may be?
Christ Jesus, it is he;
Lord Sabaoth, his name,
from age to age the same,
and he must win the battle.

And though this world, with devils filled,
should threaten to undo us,
we will not fear, for God hath willed
his truth to triumph through us.
The Prince of Darkness grim,
we tremble not for him;
his rage we can endure,
for lo, his doom is sure;
one little word shall fell him.

That word above all earthly powers,
no thanks to them, abideth;
the Spirit and the gifts are ours,
thru him who with us sideth.
Let goods and kindred go,
this mortal life also;
the body they may kill;
God's truth abideth still;
his kingdom is forever.[18]

Certainly, metaphorical battlefield illustrations are extensive throughout the psalms. Many verses describe God in warfare terminology. He is a "strong fortress to save me" (31:2); He contends and fights for us (35:1). Many times the Lord is described as a fortress as in Luther's hymn (46:11; 48:3; 62:2, 6). His strength is glorious (Ps. 93:1), He is a deliverer (Ps. 144:2), and a powerful shield (7:10;

---

[18]Martin Luther, *A Mighty Fortress is Our God* (Public domain, 1531).

144:2). He is the source of the believer's own strength (18:39). As well, David attributes literal military might and battle prowess to the Lord (18:39). Warrior enablement derives from God (18:34) and true victory comes from the Lord (55:18). Again, He battles with and for His people (24:8; 27:3; 76:3, 5).

This chapter could as well be entitled "Yahweh, Our Divine Warrior and Protector." Throughout the 150 psalms of the Bible there are countless images, illustrations, and metaphors of God as the primary agent in spiritual warfare. Psalm 18, when unpacked, has details even in its own inspired heading that helps the reader understand the context. In its introduction, 18:1, the reader learns that the psalmist is writing and expressing himself out of a situation of tremendous adversity. As further background, Psalm 18 is actually recorded previously in 2 Samuel 22. The first several verses of the psalm read:

> The LORD is my rock and my fortress and my deliverer, my God, my rock, in whom I take refuge, my shield, and the horn of my salvation, my stronghold. I call upon the LORD, who is worthy to be praised, and I am saved from my enemies. The cords of death encompassed me; the torrents of destruction assailed me; the cords of Sheol entangled me; the snares of death confronted me. In my distress I called upon the LORD; to my God I cried for help. From his temple he heard my voice, and my cry to him reached his ears" (Ps. 18:2-6).

Found in the Old Testament text, dating back to 722-931 BC, it is derived from the setting prior to the Babylonian Exile in the reign of King David. In some Bible translations, there may be a heading from the Hebrew text where verse 1 has additional information in it. Notice that it explains, "To the choirmaster. A Psalm of David, the servant of the LORD, who addressed the words of this song to the LORD on the day when the LORD delivered him from the hand of all his enemies, and from the hand of Saul. He said: I love you, O LORD, my strength."

In 2 Samuel 21, the bones of King Saul and his son Jonathan were gathered from their enemies, the Philistines, who killed and hung them. David respectfully took the bones of Saul and his dear friend Jonathan and gave them an honorable burial in the land of Benjamin in the grave of Kish, the father of Saul (21:12-14). David had been running for his life from Saul through 1 Samuel. Saul was murderously jealous of David, and David did not want to retaliate against him, but rather honored Saul as a king anointed by God.

In Psalm 18:2, just as in 2 Samuel 22, David is expressing in a song of prayer, a great expression of confidence and creativity in cataloging various military terms of defense, which he attributed to Almighty God, Yahweh, the covenant-keeping Sovereign of Israel. David, initially a shepherd that defended his sheep (in killing both lion and bear, 1 Sam. 17:34-38), then onto slaying the giant, went on to lead the team of Mighty Men of Israel in combat. He saw it absolutely necessary to rejoice in the exaltation of God through multiple descriptions of strength and strategic protection in the battles that he encountered.

As well, David spoke of the Lord in an intensely personal way. In other words, the Lord was his own personal "rock," his "fortress," and his own personal "deliverer." Looking then more closely, the following pages will unpack from 18:2, seven protective and defensive titles or terms that David used to describe Yahweh, the faithful God of Abraham, Isaac, and Jacob. Notice again, The Lord is his rock, his fortress, his deliverer, his (sheltering) rock, his shield, the horn of his salvation, and his stronghold. So, we will look briefly at each of these and remind ourselves today about our mighty God, our Fortress and our great Defender.

In the first instance, David called the Lord his *rock*. The word for rock here has a specific meaning or connotation. This is not merely a rock that one may pick up and throw into the ocean, or a paperweight. On the contrary, he was saying the Lord is his rock, He is a strategic place of protection. Literally, the word is used for a cliff or crag, a type of craggy rock. That means He is a place where David could find shelter or protection. Certainly this would have had a military connotation after David had hidden (along with his men) from the destructive efforts of Saul, the maddened king.

In Judges 20:47, the tribe of Benjamin was fleeing the tribes of Israel and their whole tribe of men ran to hide in the rock of Rimmon for 4 months. Six hundred men fled to this place in a rock and Scripture says they remained at the rock (or crag), for 4 months. The Lord was a spiritual place to flee to for David, a place where he could safely hide from the enemy. It would have been a great source of comfort with a sense of protection as well as an actual defensive position.

God Our Fortress

Again in 18:2, David calls the Lord his *fortress*, though similar in purpose a *fortress* is a little more deliberate structure of a term than, "the cleft of the rock," used just before it. A *fortress* again with the possessive pronominal indicator "my," in the Hebrew David is calling the Lord his own personal fortress. It is usually always translated *refuge* in English translations. (A synonym could be a castle or a structured stronghold.) This firm defensive structure to describe the protective power of God is used over and over by King David, as follows:

Incline your ear to me; rescue me speedily! Be a rock of refuge for me, a strong fortress to save me! For you are my rock and my fortress; and for your name's sake you lead me and guide me; you take me out of the net they have hidden for me, for you are my refuge (Ps. 31:2-4).

Also in the beloved Psalm 91, many times informally referred to as "The Soldier's Psalm" there is the illustration of the safe shelter to trust, under the protection of the Lord. "He who dwells in the shelter of the Most High will abide in the shadow of the Almighty. I will say to the LORD, "My refuge and my fortress, my God, in whom I trust" (Ps. 91:1-2).

God Our Deliverer

The next descriptive term David uses is that the Lord is his *deliverer.* Again, a statement of confidence by David, the king's personal *deliverer.* A deliverer means literally "to escape," it speaks of carrying away safely, or to cause to escape. The word also is literally "to calve" (as when a cow gives birth). It would seem that the cow is giving the calf a way to escape. The word in the context of Psalm 18:2 is of the Lord being a personal way of escape for David.

The term is found in Psalm 71:4 where the psalmist cries to the Lord, "*Rescue me,* oh my God, from the hand of the wicked" (emphasis added). Another instance to demonstrate the usage of the word is in Ezekiel, where the prophet exhorts Israel about the coming wrath of God. He warns:

They have blown the trumpet and made everything ready, but none goes to battle, for my wrath is upon all their multitude... And if any survivors *escape*, they will be on the mountains, like doves of the valleys, all of them moaning, each one over his iniquity (Ezek. 7:14, 16, emphasis added).

God is the One who brings us through trouble in life via His means of escape. He delivers His people from the effects of evil in the world or sustains them in the face of much abounding evil.

God Our Sheltering Rock

David follows in 18:2 with the expression that God is his *rock,* in whom he takes refuge. This rock though differs slightly in quality. The first rock, like a cleft or crag of a rock, could be a place of shelter/protection. In the Hebrew, the context refers to a more massive type of *rock*, a mountain or mountain stronghold. Though this differentiation is hard to define with precision, in 1 Samuel 2:2, in Hannah's prayer is voiced "there is no *rock* like our God." Again in 2 Samuel 22:32 nothing compares to this *rock*, "For who is God, but the LORD? And who is a *rock*, except our God?" One other example that helps the reader to discern this God-type rock is found in the prophecy of Habakkuk, who uses it as a title for God Himself. This rock is particularly seen here by David as a refuge. The KJV translates this portion as "my God, my strength, in whom I will trust." Here the trustworthy strength of God is expressed in distinction to the cleft or crag of the rock, as noted above.

God Our Shield

David speaking of Yahweh as a *shield* appears next. The covenant-keeping God of Israel, and the Creator God, is his personal *shield*. Literally, this defensive/protective battle weapon was also known as a "buckler." A *buckler* was a strategic type of shield. Webster's dictionary states a buckler was "composed of wood, or wickers woven together, covered with skin or leather and fortified with plates of brass or other metal, and worn on the left arm."[19] These were described as being about four feet long. Though this is the actual translation at times, my research did not conclude if this was universal and consistent with the historical time period of the Old Testament. Of course the left-handed warriors would have either needed a variation or simply rotated their buckler to suit them. Regardless, this definitely would have been a strategic portable weapon in an attack, though ostensibly quite heavy.

As well, the Hebrew word is used with the context of weaponry in 1 Chronicles 5:18 where, "The Reubenites, the Gadites, and the half-tribe of Manasseh had valiant men who carried *shield* and sword, and drew the bow, expert in war, 44,760, able to go to war"

---

[19]Noah Webster, *American Dictionary of the English Language*. 1828.

(emphasis added). Other connotations include related uses of the term, such as the word used to refer to the scaly hide of a crocodile. Furthermore, figurative uses aid in sensing the word as in Proverbs 30:5 where God, through the internalization of His Word, is referred to as a shield, "Every word of God proves true; he is a shield to those who take refuge in him."

God Our Horn of Salvation

David calls the Lord his "*horn of salvation*" next in our passage. The metaphor comes from the defensive method of wild animals that defend or protect with their horns. Most Bible commentators here refer to the nature of some of the strongest animals. That the horn of defense and protection is related here to salvation is critical as related to God saving, rescuing, delivering David. God is the One who saves and defends from ultimately all spiritual trouble too. Luke 1:68-69 cites the priest and father of John the Baptist, Zechariah, speaking prophetically of Jesus, the awaited Messiah. Here it is in the sense regarding salvation, "'Blessed be the Lord God of Israel, for he has visited and redeemed his people and has raised up a *horn of salvation* for us in the house of his servant David'" (emphasis added).

Jesus is the One who defends, saves, delivers, and has brought salvation to all who will repent and be saved. Again, the horn speaking of a power or defensive strength. Pastor/teacher John MacArthur comments about the phrase *horn of salvation*:

> Taken from the animal kingdom, a horn spoke of power, power to conquer and power to kill. When large animals go to battle, they go to battle using their horns. The large, powerful beasts conquer and kill with their horns. So the horn became the symbol of conquering, killing power. And that's the way they viewed the Messiah. The Messiah is going to come and conquer and destroy the enemy and set His people free. He's going to be the great deliverer, the great rescuer.

And you see that...that horn concept, as I said, in many places in the Old Testament.

In Deuteronomy 33:17, Joseph is being spoken of here and he speaks of Joseph as a firstborn of his ox. "Majesty is his and his horns are the horns of the wild ox. With them he shall push the peoples all at once to the ends of the earth." So they saw like this great ox, lowering its horns and just driving people out. And that's how they viewed the coming of Messiah. He would come, and with great power like a massive formidable animal, literally drive the enemies out and destroy them and rescue God's people. This is what thrilled him, their impending deliverance.[20]

Thus, David expresses in Psalm 18:2 that Yahweh, the covenant-keeping God of Israel, is such a mighty and powerful horn of salvation.

God Our Stronghold

Lastly, King David exalts Yahweh as his personal stronghold, and certainly, the people of God would have echoed this in reading, singing, and meditating on the ancient psalms. This great confidence that David was voicing is that God Almighty is an impenetrable stronghold. A stronghold here speaks of someplace (figuratively) that is a refuge, security, a secure height, a high tower. The term is translated by the KJV at times as a *high tower*, and Isaiah 25:12 speaks of such unassailable fortifications, or "The fortress of the high fort of thy walls" (KJV). Indeed, God is our place of safety and defense.

---

[20]John MacArthur, "Zachariah's Song of Salvation: Introduction," *Grace to You*. https://www.gty.org/resources/sermons/42-16/zachariahs-song-of-salvation-introduction.

In the 1639 work *The Righteous Man's Tower* by Puritan Jeremiah Dyke, Dyke reflects illustratively of our great need to rely on the security of God as our high tower in times of trouble. He writes:

> If a man do run to a tower, yet if that be a weak an insufficient tower, without men and munition, and a ruinous shaken tower; or if a man do make choice of a tower, a strong sufficient tower, yet if in his danger he betake not himself to that tower but he sit still; or if he sit not still, yet he but only go and walk on easily towards it, he may well be met withal, and a danger may arrest him, surprise him, and cut him off before he get to the tower over his head. But the man that will be safe, as he must choose a strong tower, so he must go, nay, run into that tower. Running will not secure a man unless the tower is strong.[21]

In concluding, my prayer is that these meditations on the protective and defensive power of our God would grant the reader greater confidence in God and that the believer will take heart in the uncertainty and evil times in which we live today. David trusted in God as his great defender and he was called by God as "a man after his own heart" (1 Sam. 13:14).

---

[21]Charles H. Spurgeon, *The Treasury of David*. (Public Domain, 1869), Vol. 1, 252.

Questions for Spiritual Formation:

1. Why is the psalmist's continual use of strong, defensive, and protective (often military) type illustrations comforting to the human heart? What comforts come to mind with such imagery?

2. How is it reassuring that over 3,000 years ago King David sang and prayed in this way, a way that is equally applicable to believers today?

3. At what times in your life have you prayed or sought God in this way, running to Him as your fortress, and refuge?

Our God, our Help in Ages Past
by Isaac Watts

Our God, our help in ages past,
our hope for years to come,
our shelter from the stormy blast,
and our eternal home:

Under the shadow of your throne
your saints have dwelt secure;
sufficient is your arm alone,
and our defense is sure.

Before the hills in order stood
or earth received its frame,
from everlasting you are God,
to endless years the same.

A thousand ages in your sight
are like an evening gone,
short as the watch that ends the night
before the rising sun.

Time, like an ever-rolling stream,
soon bears us all away;
we fly forgotten, as a dream
dies at the opening day.[22]

---

[22]Isaac Watts, *Our God, Our Help in Ages Past*, (Public Domain, 1719).

Chapter 4

Battle Preparedness

A Devotional from the Pages of the Patriarchs

Take heed, then, often to come together to give thanks to God, and show forth His praise. For when ye come frequently together in the same place, the powers of Satan are destroyed, and his 'fiery darts' (Eph. 6:16) urging to sin fall back ineffectual. For your concord and harmonious faith prove his destruction, and the torment of his assistants. Nothing is better than that peace which is according to Christ, by which all war, both of aerial and terrestrial spirits, is brought to an end. 'For we wrestle not against blood and flesh, but against principalities and powers, and against the rulers of the darkness of this world, against spiritual wickedness in heavenly places.' (Eph. 6:12)[23]

This chapter includes encouraging reflections from church history on themes of spiritual warfare and the Christian life. The history of the early church is filled with life, insights, and untold valuable lessons. A perusing of the writings of the Ante-Nicene Fathers (early Christian leaders who lived and wrote prior to the Council of

---

[23]Ignatius, Chap. XIII, Exhortation to Meet Together Frequently for the Worship of God. 1.13, *The Ante-Nicene Fathers: Translations of the Writings of the Fathers Down to A.D. 325*. Edited by Alexander Roberts and James Donaldson. 10 vols. 1885–1887, Public Domain.

Nicaea AD 325, hereafter *ANF,*) contains much benefit for the believer. From this age where the historically formative Nicene Creed[24] was written, the Nicene fathers and the post-Nicene fathers (written during and beyond the era of the Nicene Council) lend a treasure from the lives of early believers that is tremendously applicable and valuable today.

The selected quotes that are included in this piece on themes surrounding faith in the spiritual war around us have varying contexts but show a universal perspective from early Christian leaders that God is our defense. As well, these moving and earnest snapshots of the early Christian leaders demonstrate that God has given us true weapons for the good fight of the faith. From Ignatius (AD 35-108) comes his exhortations for Christians to embrace the struggle of life in the faith God has given to them. He has left an inheritance of devotional truth for the believer today, admonishing the saints to band

---

[24]**The Nicene Creed**

I believe in one God, the Father Almighty, Maker of heaven and earth, and of all things visible and invisible.

And in one Lord Jesus Christ, the only-begotten Son of God, begotten of the Father before all worlds; God of God, Light of Light, very God of very God; begotten, not made, being of one substance with the Father, by whom all things were made.

Who, for us men and for our salvation, came down from heaven, and was incarnate by the Holy Spirit of the virgin Mary, and was made man; and was crucified also for us under Pontius Pilate; He suffered and was buried; and the third day He rose again, according to the Scriptures; and ascended into heaven, and sits on the right hand of the Father; and He shall come again, with glory, to judge the quick and the dead; whose kingdom shall have no end.

And I believe in the Holy Ghost, the Lord and Giver of Life; who proceeds from the Father and the Son; who with the Father and the Son together is worshipped and glorified; who spoke by the prophets.

And I believe in one holy catholic and apostolic Church. I acknowledge one baptism for the remission of sins; and I look for the resurrection of the dead, and the life of the world to come. Amen.

together through the storms of life, as an army of spiritual warriors who are more than adequately prepared for the battle. He writes:

> Labour together with one another; strive in company together; run together; suffer together; sleep together; and awake together, as the stewards, and associates, and servants of God. Please ye Him under whom ye fight, and from whom ye shall receive your wages. Let none of you be found a deserter. Let your baptism endure as your arms; your faith as your helmet; your love as your spear; your patience as a complete panoply. Let your works be the charge assigned to you, that you may obtain for them a most worthy recompense. Be long-suffering, therefore, with one another, in meekness, and God shall be so with you. [25]

Of course, the words of the early fathers are not equal in quality to the inerrant and inspired Word of the Bible, but the believer finds in them sobriety and devotion to the gospel that far surpasses what is often today presented as the Christian faith in the world. The reader of this book can benefit from meditating on both the content of these early writings, but also their fierce perspective of the battle that surrounds us.

The writings of the Ante-Nicene Fathers (*ANF*) have the intriguing characteristic of overlapping in time with the lives of the apostles, which would give further explanation as to their vast quantity of biblical concepts and ideas woven into their writings. It is attested (and perhaps embellished) that Ignatius was a child during the days of the apostles and lived simultaneously in the life and times of the beloved early church leader Polycarp.[26] Amazingly,

---

[25]Ignatius, Exhortation to Meet Together, (*ANF*, Public Domain), 1.13.

[26]Edward D. Andrews, *Early Christianity in the First Century: Jesus Witnesses to the Ends of the Earth*, (Cambridge, OH: Christian Publishing House, 2017), 82. "The seductive myth which represents this Father as the little child whom the Lord placed in the midst of his apostles (Matt. 18:2) indicates at

dating around AD 30-107, is found clear biographical details into the life of our good brother Ignatius. The historian Phillip Shaff again captures the historical context:

> Supposing the letters of Ignatius and the account of his martyrdom to be authentic, we learn from them that he voluntarily presented himself before Trajan at Antioch, the seat of his bishopric, when that prince was on his *first* expedition against the Parthians and Armenians (A.D. 107); and on professing himself a Christian, was condemned to the wild beasts. After a long and dangerous voyage, he came to Smyrna, of which Polycarp was bishop, and thence wrote his four Epistles to the Ephesians, the Magnesians, the Trallians, and the Romans. From Smyrna he came to Troas, and tarrying there a few days, he wrote to the Philadelphians, the Smyrnaeans, and Polycarp. He then came on to Neapolis, and passed through the whole of Macedonia. Finding a ship at Dyrrachium in Epirus about to sail into Italy, he embarked, and crossing the Adriatic, was brought to Rome, where he perished on the 20th of December 107, or, as some think, who deny a twofold expedition of Trajan against the Parthians, on the same day of the year A.D. 116.[27]

Again, we can see the early leaders were immersed in Scripture, and their writings are saturated with biblical concepts and applications. Further examples come to us from the early leader, Barnabas, who was also steeped in the perspective of the seriousness

---

least the period when he may be supposed to have been born. That he and Polycarp were fellow-disciples under St. John, is a tradition by no means inconsistent with anything in the Epistles of either. His subsequent history is sufficiently indicated in the Epistles which follow. From the Introductory Note to the Epistle of Ignatius to the Ephesians."

[27]*Introductory Note to the Epistle of Ignatius to the Ephesians*, (*ANF*, Public Domain).

of the Christian fight in this world. The believer can be reminded here of New Testament portions of the epistles of Peter and Paul. Barnabas wrote:

> Since, therefore, the days are evil, and Satan possesses the power of this world, we ought to give heed to ourselves, and diligently inquire into the ordinances of the Lord. Fear and patience, then, are helpers of our faith; and long-suffering and continence are things which fight on our side.[28,29]

Many others of the patristic period (ante-Nicene, Nicene, post-Nicene fathers) reflect a similar perspective of the rigorous spiritual life, facing adversity, persecution, and much spiritual opposition. This would include what they believed to be demonic and hostile activity against the Kingdom of God.

As the back story to Clement, consider this portion from his biographical information compiled by Shaff in the ante-Nicene writings:

> [AD 30-100] Clement was probably a Gentile and a Roman. He seems to have been at Philippi with St. Paul in AD 57

---

[28] *The Epistle of Barnabas*, (*ANF*, Public Domain), 1.0.02.

[29] Intro note to the Epistle of Barnabas, (*ANF*, Public Domain), "[AD 100.] The writer of this Epistle is supposed to have been an Alexandrian Jew of the times of Trajan and Hadrian. He was a layman; but possibly he bore the name of "Barnabas," and so has been confounded with his holy and apostolic namesire. It is more probable that the Epistle, being anonymous, was attributed to St. Barnabas, by those who supposed that apostle to be the author of the Epistle to the Hebrews, and who discovered similarities in the plan and purpose of the two works... When it is remembered that no one ascribes the Epistle to the apostolic Barnabas till the times of Clement of Alexandria, and that it is ranked by Eusebius among the "spurious" writings, which, however much known and read in the Church, were never regarded as authoritative, little doubt can remain that the external evidence is of itself weak, and should not make us hesitate for a moment in refusing to ascribe this writing to Barnabas the Apostle."

when that first-born of the Western churches was passing through great trials of faith. There, with holy women and others, he ministered to the apostle and to the saints. As this city was a Roman colony, we need not inquire how a Roman happened to be there. He was possibly in some public service, and it is not improbable that he had visited Corinth in those days. From the apostle, and his companion, St. Luke, he had no doubt learned the use of the Septuagint, in which his knowledge of the Greek tongue soon rendered him an adept. His copy of that version, however, does not always agree with the Received Text, as the reader will perceive.

After the death of the apostles...Clement was the natural representative of St. Paul, and even of his companion, the "apostle of the circumcision;" and naturally he wrote the Epistle in the name of the local church, when brethren looked to them for advice. St. John, no doubt, was still surviving at Patmos or in Ephesus; but the Philippians, whose intercourse with Rome is attested by the visit of Epaphroditus, looked naturally to the surviving friends of their great founder; nor was the aged apostle in the East equally accessible...

Clement fell asleep, probably soon after he dispatched his letter. It is the legacy of one who reflects the apostolic age in all the beauty and evangelical truth which were the first-fruits of the Spirit's presence with the Church. He shares with others the aureole of glory attributed by St. Paul (Phi. 4:3), 'His name is in the Book of Life.'"[30,]

---

[30]Introductory Note to the First Epistle of Clement to the Corinthians, (*ANF*, Public Domain), "A co-presbyter with Linus and Cletus, he succeeded them in the government of the Roman Church. I have reluctantly adopted the opinion that his Epistle was written near the close of his life, and not just after the persecution of Nero. It is not improbable that Linus and Cletus both perished in that fiery trial, and that Clement's immediate succession to their work and place occasions the chronological difficulties of that period... All roads pointed

According to the biographical account by Shaff, Clement was a church leader and that seems to have followed in carrying on the work of "Linus and Cletus," who may well have perished under the persecutions of Nero. Clearly considering the time period will remind us of the distinct adversity that he and his contemporaries would have faced. His thoughts demonstrate a warrior mindset when referring to the fierce determination of persevering in the faith.

Likewise, Clement, writing from Rome, speaks of the great purposes of God in gathering for war His "soldiers of peace," giving to us wonderful and heavy warfare imagery of the end goal of our fight—to glorify the Prince of Peace who fought hell for us at the cross and won the victory for us through His atonement and resurrection. Clement wrote:

> But it has been God's fixed and constant purpose to save the flock of men: for this end the good God sent the good Shepherd. And the Word, having unfolded the truth, showed to men the height of salvation, that either repenting they might be saved, or refusing to obey, they might be judged. This is the proclamation of righteousness: to those that obey, glad tidings; to those that disobey, judgment. The loud trumpet, when sounded, collects the soldiers, and proclaims war. And shall not Christ, breathing a strain of peace to the ends of the earth, gather together His own soldiers, the soldiers of

---

towards the Imperial City, and started from its *Milliarium Aureum*. But, though Clement doubtless wrote the letter, he conceals his own name, and puts forth the brethren, who seem to have met in council, and sent a brotherly delegation (Chap. lix.). The entire absence of the spirit of Diotrephes (3 Jn 1:9), and the close accordance of the Epistle, in humility and meekness, with that of St. Peter (1 Pt 5:1-5), are noteworthy features. The whole will be found animated with the loving and faithful spirit of St. Paul's dear Philippians, among whom the writer had learned the Gospel."

peace?...."Let us array ourselves in the armour of peace, putting on the breastplate of righteousness, and taking the shield of faith, and binding our brows with the helmet, of salvation; and the sword of the Spirit, which is the word of God," (Eph. 6:14-17) let us sharpen. So the apostle in the spirit of peace commands. These are our invulnerable weapons: armed with these, let us face the evil one; "the fiery darts of the evil one" let us quench with the sword-points dipped in water, that, have been baptized by the Word.[31]

Furthermore, considering how they lived and died, much in the context of extreme opposition to the Christian faith, this reminds the modern pilgrim that the catalyst of persecution and suffering has at times been authorized by our heavenly Father who works all things out for the good "to those who love God, who are called according to *His* purpose" (Rom. 8:28, NASB). It is at times overwhelming to reflect upon how early brothers, sisters, mothers, and fathers in Christ were treated poorly and often violently in this fallen world. Yet, one can be assured that in the same way, and to the furthest extent, Christ Jesus experienced worse treatment from the hands of sinful men in the darkness of this world.

Again, Shaff brings,

From one commentary, a North African Bishop of the 3rd Century, comes stern exhortation against apostasy from God. He admonishes Christians that even death is superior to compromise of the coward and deserter that neglects or rejects advocacy for the message of Christ crucified and resurrected.[32]

---

[31]Clement of Alexandria, *Exhortation to the Heathen*, (*ANF*, Public Domain), 2.11.

[32][AD 240] Our author seems to have been a North-African bishop, of whom little is known save what we learn from his own writings. He has been supposed to incline to some ideas of Praxes, and also to the Millenarians, but perhaps on

This alluded to ancient bishop describes further exhortation for early saints, but also this unquestionably applies to the church today. Let the believer today pray that he or she would never succumb to such apostasy that would compromise the eternal gospel of Christ. He writes:

> Moreover, when war is waged, or an enemy attacks, if one be able either to conquer or to be hidden, they are great trophies; but unhappy will he be who shall be taken by them. He noses country and king who has been unwilling to fight worthily for the truth, for his country, or for life. He ought to die rather than go under a barbarian king; and let him seek slavery who is willing to transfer himself to enemies without law... It will be an infamous thing if any one declares himself to the enemy. He who knows not how to conquer, and runs to deliver himself up, has weakly foregone praise for neither his own nor his country's good. Then he was unwilling to live, since life itself will perish. If anyone is without God, or profane from the enemy, they are become as sounding brass, or deaf as adders: such men ought abundantly to pray or to hide themselves.[33]

Again from the theme concerning those who had apostatized or deserted the Lord. The theme reflects the intense climate of pressure to reject the faith in the early days of the church. Cyprian writes of the spiritual battle at hand and the hostility that the early believers faced. Here differentiating the believers from the apostate and recognizing the battle of accepting martyrdom for Christ:

---

insufficient grounds. His Millenarianism reflects the views of a very primitive age, and that without the corrupt Chiliasm of a later period, which brought about a practical repudiation of the whole system.

[33]Commondianus, The Instructions of Commondianus in Favor of Christian Discipline, (ANF, Public Domain), 4.50.

We should make a difference, dearest brother, between those who either have apostatized, and, having returned to the world which they have renounced, are living heathenish lives, or, having become deserters to the heretics, are daily taking up parricidal arms against the Church.[34]

Cyprian here describes those who had been "prepared for the battle." Facing the ultimate battle of being martyred for their faith in Christ is being described, stating how Cyprian terms "granting peace" for those persecuted in a hostile means, some unto death. The warfare here taking on then a slightly different connotation, but the sense is understood that some of the early Christians endured a type of "warfare" of being tortured and brought to the edge of martyrdom and some forced to their death being tried extensively to break them and cause them to deny the Master. The early church leader writes:

We grant peace, not for rest, but for the field of battle. If, according to what we hear, and desire, and believe of them, they shall stand bravely, and shall overthrow the adversary with us in the encounter, we shall not repent of having granted peace to men so brave. Yea, it is the great honour and glory of our episcopate to have granted peace to martyrs, so that we, as priests, who daily celebrate the sacrifices of God, may prepare offerings and victims for God. But if — which may the Lord avert from our brethren — any one of the lapsed should deceive, seeking peace by guile, and at the time of the impending struggle receiving peace without any purpose of doing battle, he betrays and deceives himself, hiding one thing in his heart and pronouncing another with his voice. We, so far as it is allowed to us to see and to judge, look upon the face of each one; we are not able to scrutinize the heart and to inspect the mind. Concerning these the Discerner and Searcher of hidden things judges, and He will quickly come

---

[34]Cyprian, *The Epistles of Cyprian*, (*ANF*, Public Domain), 5.02.53.03.

and judge of the secrets and hidden things of the heart. But the evil ought not to stand in the way of the good, but rather the evil ought to be assisted by the good. Neither is peace, therefore, to be denied to those who are about to endure martyrdom, because there are some who will refuse it, since for this purpose peace should be granted to all who are about to enter upon the warfare.[35]

Cyprian admonished the early believers to heed his warning of extreme adversity and hardship of their times. He brought another connotation that the early Christians were to face in the persecutions. He spoke of fighting and battling that would be the manner of enduring the time of Antichrist that they were encountering. From his writings are found passionate expressions encouraging the early Christians to prepare for the adversity they would suffer. He wrote:

> For you ought to know and to believe, and hold it for certain, that the day of affliction has begun to hang over our heads, and the end of the world and the time of Antichrist to draw near, so that we all must stand prepared for the battle; nor consider anything but the glory of life eternal, and the crown of the confession of the Lord; and not regard those things which are coming as being such as were those which have passed away.[36]

Here Cyprian seems empathetic with the early flock of believers of his day, he knew many would suffer, some unto death. He even referred to verses (as found in the quote below) that may not necessarily be seen as applying to harsh persecution in their written context by Western Christians today, but would have been felt to apply to the waves of suffering and persecution that were occurring during his day. For example, he added:

---

[35]Ibid, 5.02.53.03.
[36]Cyprian, *Epistles*, (*ANF*, Public Domain), 5.08.50.01.

A severer and a fiercer fight is now threatening, for which the soldiers of Christ ought to prepare themselves with uncorrupted faith and robust courage, considering that they drink the cup of Christ's blood daily. For the reason that they themselves may also be able to shed their blood for Christ. For this is to wish to be found with what Christ both taught and did, according to the Apostle John, who said, "He that saith he abideth in Christ, ought himself also so as to walk even as he walked." (1 Jn. 2:6) Moreover, the blessed Apostle Paul exhorts and teaches, saying, "We are God's children; but if children, then heirs of God, and joint-heirs with Christ; if so be that we suffer with Him, that we may also be glorified together (Ro. 8:16-17).[37]

Again, Cyprian applied fully living for Christ, even "shedding one's blood for Christ" as part of the deepest experiences of the Christian pilgrimage. He writes pastorally, with much warmth and compassion for the sheep of the Lord Jesus whose lives would have been filled with many bodily afflictions in the times of harsh persecution that were occurring. He adds another feature to their fighting, stating that their battle would be won with "the strength of patience." He wrote:

It behooves us, in this bodily frailty and weakness, always to struggle and to fight. And this struggle and encounter cannot be sustained but by the strength of patience. But as we are to be examined and searched out, diverse sufferings are introduced; and a manifold kind of temptations is inflicted by the losses of property, by the heats of fevers, by the torments of wounds, by the loss of those dear to us. Nor does anything distinguish between the unrighteous and the righteous more,

[37]Cyprian, *Epistles*, (*ANF*, Public Domain), 5.08.50.01.

than that in affliction the unrighteous man impatiently complains and blasphemes, while the righteous is proved by his patience, as it is written: 'In pain endure, and in thy low estate have patience; for gold and silver are tried in the fire' (Sirach 2:4, 5).[38]

The church today must take on the mantle of the early church fathers. Their writings are a goldmine of wisdom, history, and insight. There is much to gain and much blessing to miss if the early church fathers are overlooked as insignificant or irrelevant. Wisdom would gather in as much from Christians throughout history and discern what, if anything, should be discarded and of what should be cherished and meditated upon. "Do not despise prophecies, but test everything; hold fast what is good" (1 Thess. 5:20-21).

---

[38]Cyprian, *The Treatise of Cyprian*, (*ANF*, Public Domain). 5.09.17.

Questions for Spiritual Formation:

1. In what ways is it compelling to read the words of early Christian church leaders (even in considering their lives may have overlapped with the apostles)?

2. In what ways are the spirituality, suffering, and adversity of these early church leaders alien to our own experiences as twenty-first century Christians in the West? What are some similarities with Christians today?

3. What can we take home from the contemplation of the lives of the Christians in the Catacombs of Rome? In what ways are they similar to the experiences of the Secret Church Christians today?

When Morning Gilds the Skies

"When morning gilds the skies, my heart awaking cries:
May Jesus Christ be praised!
Alike at work and prayer, To Jesus I repair;
May Jesus Christ be praised!

Does sadness fill my mind? A solace here I find,
May Jesus Christ be praised!
Or fades my earthly bliss? My comfort still is this,
May Jesus Christ be praised!

When sleep her balm denies, my silent spirit sighs,
May Jesus Christ be praised!
When evil thoughts molest, with this I shield my breast:
May Jesus Christ be praised!

The night becomes as day, when from the heart we say:
May Jesus Christ be praised!
The pow'rs of darkness fear, when this sweet chant they hear:
May Jesus Christ be praised!

In heav'n's eternal bliss, the loveliest strain is this,
May Jesus Christ be praised!
Let earth, and sea, and sky, from depth to height reply,
May Jesus Christ be praised!

Be this, while life is mine, my song of love divine:
May Jesus Christ be praised!
Sing this eternal song, through all the ages long:
May Jesus Christ be praised!"[39]

---

[39]Anonymous, *When Morning Gilds the Skies* (1744, Public Domain).

Chapter 5

Spiritual Combat:

Guidance from the Era of the Puritans

"Puritans saw themselves as God's pilgrims traveling home, God's warriors battling against the world, the flesh and the devil; and servants under orders to do all the good they could as they went along,"- J.I. Packer [40]

This chapter derives from the mindset of the Puritans, who wrote much on combatting against evil and sin in the trenches of defending the very truth of the living God. In the writings of the Puritans is found a twofold nature to the gospel influence in the life of the believer. Firstly, as a characteristic of spiritual warfare, the saint must resolve to pursue and is certainly compelled by God to move towards an inner fortification of transforming grace. The Puritans championed an authentic and biblical meditation that may be described as a vital component in the theme of sanctification.

Secondly, an outward assertion of faith in advancement of the Kingdom message of Christ crucified is found often in Puritan writings. This Puritan apologetic, or defense of biblical truth, is also an innate characteristic of Puritan era literature. Just as the believer

---

[40]J. I. Packer, *Collected Shorter Writings of J. I. Packer: Honouring the People of God, vol. 4* (Carlisle: Paternoster Press, 1999), 24-5.

is immersed in a sin-cursed world and in an active and hostile climate in the world (Eph. 6:12), so the Puritans offer light and aid for the Christian journey.

Forging an Inner Fortification of
Holiness, Prayer, and Meditation

Again, the first prong of help from the wider body of Puritan writing is that of the inner fortification opposing the world, the flesh, and the devil. This is sought by an inner consecration and application of the spiritual disciplines in daily life. Three ways in which this God-focused resolve—or fortification of the inner man— denotes the very internalization of a posture of spiritual warfare are:

> 1) the self-confrontation of godless and adversarial thought patterns;
> 2) the impetus to engage in diligent prayer; and
> 3) the meditation that cultivates biblical transformation.

The Self-Confrontation of Godless
and Adversarial Thought Patterns

Concerning the first way of cultivating this type of Godward discipline, consider first the Scriptures. The Bible teaches us to take "every thought captive to the obedience of Christ" (2 Cor. 10:5, NASB). Therefore, the inner life is often the seat of conflict that is in our hearts, the very place where we habitually ignore the truth that leads us closer to the Lord. Thus, to take every thought captive is to wage war on wickedness in the realm of the heart and mind.

It involves the assessment and examination of the self. Scripture advocates the practice of a biblical, yet not overly introspective, self-evaluation. At one level, the professing Christian is to confirm his or her faith through an open and honest self-examination. In 2 Corinthians 13:5, Paul instructed the Corinthian Church to "Examine yourselves, to see whether you are in the faith. Test yourselves. Or do you not realize this about yourselves, that Jesus Christ is in you? — unless indeed you fail to meet the test!" Yet as well, the believer is routinely to engage in a work of self-examination, not to merit salvation by any means, but to affirm the saving knowledge of Christ and the maintenance of a functioning and cleansed conscience.

The communion table is the reoccurring celebration of examining one's own heart in light of the work of Christ. Again, though at an earlier date, Paul instructed the Corinthian Church:

> Whoever, therefore, eats the bread or drinks the cup of the Lord in an unworthy manner will be guilty concerning the body and blood of the Lord. Let a person examine himself, then, and so eat of the bread and drink of the cup. For anyone who eats and drinks without discerning the body eats and drinks judgment on himself. That is why many of you are weak and ill, and some have died. But if we judged ourselves truly, we would not be judged (1 Cor. 11:27-31).

The saint, a justified sinner, should certainly sense the responsibility to not only assess the activity of the mind and conscience rightly, but also to deal swiftly with inner corruption—both in the activity of confession to God directly (1 John 1:9), and subsequently to maintain a transparent community of faith in the local church where there is a healthy bearing of one another's burdens in confession and prayer. James teaches the early Christians to "confess your sins to one another and pray for one another" (James 5:16).

An ongoing assessment of the inner life is to be a well-formed habit in the believer. The Puritans taught this thoroughly in their appeal for Christians to cultivate and understand the human conscience. A knowledge and righteous test of one's conscience is the path to self-examination when we arrive at the Lord's Table. In the robust volume   entitled *A Puritan Theology,* Beeke and Jones write:

...the Puritans sometimes appealed to the word *conscience* itself. They argued that conscience is derived from two Latin words: Scientia, which means 'knowledge', and con, a prefix implying community or joint sharing in something- in this case, knowledge shared jointly with God, or knowledge of us that God shares with us. [41]

Furthermore, the conscience must always be healthy and cultivated through the investment of biblical knowledge. It could be established through biblical reasoning then that the conscience could become corrupt or self-deceived without the continual influence of godliness in the life of the believer. Paul instructs the Corinthian believers that some must be protected from becoming defiled in their consciences if they are influenced by things they are not mature enough to practice discernment about.

He says that the more mature may be guilty toward the lesser mature by "wounding their conscience" (1 Cor. 8:12). Again, "A Puritan Theology" explains, "...the Puritans taught that the conscience functions as a spiritual nervous system..."[42] Clearly, the saint must be diligent to be a counselor unto himself or herself that he or she may maintain a healthy conscience before other believers and all men, just as Paul was able to boast about to the glory of God. In 2 Corinthians 1:12, Paul states, "For our boast is this, the testimony of our conscience, that we behaved in the world with simplicity and godly sincerity, not by earthly wisdom but by the grace of God, and supremely so toward you."

The Impetus to Engage in Diligent Prayer

The impetus to engage in diligent prayer is an assertion of spiritual warfare that reflects the life of the inner man. The prayer

---

[41]Beeke and Jones, *A Puritan Theology: Doctrine for Life*, (Grand Rapids: Reformation Heritage Books, 2012), 911.

[42]Ibid, 912.

warrior then must understand the ferocity that he or she is called to through the heavenly commission to prayer. (e.g., 1 Thess. 5:17: "Pray without ceasing") Christians throughout history have learned to humbly walk in the Christian life with increasing knowledge of the power of prayer.

From the Puritan era, John Bunyan among others wrote much on the weightiness of prayer. In Puritanical fashion, Bunyan entitled the book he wrote on prayer:

> I will pray with the Spirit and with understanding also, or A Discourse touching prayer; wherein is discovered, I) what prayer is, II) What it is to pray with the Spirit, III) What it is to pray with the Spirit and with understanding also., spiritually enlightened to see the promises and to be encouraged.[43]

Often Puritan writers sought to write comprehensively and with great piety, yet with theological and practical precision.

In the classic work, Bunyan writes a thesis statement that brings definition to prayer. He states,

> Prayer is a sincere, sensible, affectionate pouring out of the heart or soul to God, through Christ, in the strength and assistance of the Holy Spirit, for such things as God hath promised, or according to the Word, for the good of the church, with submission, in faith, to the will of God.[44]

Prayer and this posture of spiritual warfare mindedness are inextricably linked because "the weapons of our warfare are not of the flesh" (2 Cor. 10:4), but are rather spiritual weaponry.

---

[43] John Bunyan, *I Will Pray with the Spirit AND With the Understanding Also- O R, A Discourse Touching Prayer; Wherein is discovered, I. What Prayer Is. II. What It Is To Pray With The Spirit. III. What It Is To Pray With The Spirit A N D With the U N D E R S T A N D I N G also...spiritually enlightened to see the promises and to be encouraged,* (Public Domain, 1663).

[44] Ibid.

The prayer warrior is offered a mentorship to pray throughout the Bible. This mentorship ranges from the civil corporate invocations of King Solomon (1 Kings 8:22-52) for the dedication of the temple, to the corporate prayer of repentance of Ezra the priest—as he and everyone "who trembled at the words of the God of Israel...gathered around" (Ezra 9:4, 6-7)—to the high priestly prayer of the Lord Jesus who interceded mightily for those who would believe in Him through the words testified by the early saints (John 17:20). Prayer is the battle cry of the Christian soldier, it is the heart longing to approach the throne of grace with confidence for the full supply of mercy and grace needed for enduring the battle at hand (Heb. 4:16).

One practical example of the effort of prayer in spiritual warfare is the advancement of the gospel in world missions. We are arrogant if we presume that missions will be accomplished on the striving of raw human energy. It is evermore the sovereign grace of God that is the current in which the ministry of missions flows, and prayer is the heavenward movement that works forth the eternal purposes of the Kingdom of God.

The bedrock of the Reformation Creeds and Catechisms were greatly relied upon by those of the Puritan era. Question 191 of the Westminister Larger Catechism asks about the Lord's Prayer, "What do we pray for in the second petition?" and that petition reads, "Thy Kingdom Come." (Matt. 6:10). And the catechism provides the reader with an answer to the question, which wonderfully reads:

> In the second petition, (which is, *Thy kingdom come*) acknowledging ourselves and all mankind to be by nature under the dominion of sin and Satan, we pray, that the kingdom of sin and Satan may be destroyed, the gospel propagated throughout the world, the Jews called, the fullness of the Gentiles brought in; the church furnished with all gospel-officers and ordinances, purged from corruption, countenanced and maintained by the civil magistrate: that the ordinances of Christ may be purely dispensed, and made effectual to the

converting of those that are yet in their sins, and the confirm-ing, comforting, and building up of those that are already converted that Christ would rule in our hearts here, and has-ten the time of his second coming, and our reigning with him forever and that he would be pleased so to exercise the king-dom of his power in all the world, as may best conduce to these ends.[45]

The missiological retort to the catechesis answer of Q. 191 would have been foundational in the most mature Puritan congrega-tions and communities. Historically there is evidence of this from the pre-Puritan Calvinistic missions (to include the French Huguenot missionary efforts to the area that is now Brazil).[46] The effort to bring the gospel to Brazil by the Reformation era efforts was limited, from Geneva, "John Calvin sent two Protestant pastors to accompany a Protestant expedition to Brazil in 1556. Upon arrival, however, the leader of the expedition betrayed the settlers, and the project was abandoned."[47]

Regarding the early Puritan era missionaries to the Native Americans (which are the best examples of the influence of the

---

[45] WLC, Q. 191.

[46] The Huguenot Society of America, Huguenot History, http://www.hu-guenotsocietyofamerica.org/?page=Huguenot-History, "The Huguenots were French Protestants. The tide of the Reformation reached France early in the six-teenth century and was part of the religious and political fomentation of the times. It was quickly embraced by members of the nobility, by the intellectual elite, and by professionals in trades, medicine, and crafts. It was a respectable movement involving the most responsible and accomplished people of France. It signified their desire for greater freedom religiously and politically…"

[47] Thomas S. Giles, "Columbus and Christianity: Did You Know?," *Christian History Institute*, https://christianhistoryinstitute.org/magazine/arti-cle/columbus-and-christianity-did-you-know.

European expansion and colonialism), there are good models to consider.[48] Examples to ponder include the later Great Awakening - American Puritans that served nobly in reaching the Native Americans with compassion like David Brainerd and Jonathan Edwards.

In the travels of David Brainerd to labor with extraordinary diligence towards the compassionate evangelization of the Indians and further discipleship of the Native American communities, Brainerd prayed for the hand of God upon their lives, work, health, and physical protection. From his diary we read:

> Tues, October 9, 1744. We rose about four in the morning, and commending ourselves to God by prayer, and asking his special protection, we set out on our journey homewards about five, and traveled with great steadiness till past six at night; and then made us a fire, and a shelter of barks, and so rested. I had some clear and comfortable thoughts on a divine subject, by the way, towards night. — In the night the wolves howled around us; but God preserved us.

---

[48]Matthew Vogan, John Elliot: Puritan Missionary to the Indians, *Evangelical Times*, http://www.evangelical-times.org/archive/item/447/Historical/John-Eliot--Puritan-Missionary-to-the-Indians/, "The Puritans were deeply committed to missionary endeavour. All the well-known Puritan and Covenanting ministers subscribed to a petition presented to parliament in 1641 'for the propagating of the gospel in America and the West Indies'. The best example of this spirit was to be found in New England. The Massachusetts Bay Company's Charter of 1628 stated that one of the chief purposes of establishing the colony was 'to win and invite the natives of the country to the knowledge and obedience of the only true God and Saviour of mankind'. The seal of the colony depicted a North American Indian saying, 'Come over and help us' (Acts 16:9). The settlers needed the strength of believing resolve - in 'the Virginia massacre' of 1622 four hundred colonists had been slaughtered. The call brought 15,000 individuals to the shores of New England between 1627 and 1640 - among them the most famous of Puritan missionaries, John Eliot."

The next day they rose early, and set forward, and traveled that day till they came to an Irish settlement, with which Mr. Brainerd was acquainted, and lodged there. He speaks of some sweetness in divine things, and thankfulness to God for his goodness to him in this journey, though attended with shame for his barrenness. On Thursday he continued in the same place; and both he and Mr. Byram preached there to the people.

Friday, Oct. 12, 1744. Rode home to my lodgings; where I poured out my soul to God in secret prayer, and endeavored to bless him for his abundant goodness to me in my late journey. I scarce ever enjoyed more health, at least, of later years; and God marvelously, and almost miraculously, supported me under the fatigues of the way, and traveling on foot. Blessed be the Lord, who continually preserves me in all my ways." On Saturday he went again to the Irish settlement, to spend the Sabbath there, his Indians being gone."[49]

We are blessed today to have the heartfelt, prayer-filled memoirs of the missionary David Brainerd.

The Meditation That Cultivates Biblical Transformation

There is absolutely a biblical meditation that cultivates true life transformation. In Puritan style, I initially entitled this section, "The fortification of the inner man through gospel meditation upon themes of true sanctification and true biblical transformation," but instead included it as a thesis statement for the section. The description of this genuine meditation is found throughout Scripture, but one specific example is found in Psalm 119:11 where the psalmist expresses, "I have stored up your word in my heart, that I might not sin

---

[49]Jonathan Edwards, *The Diary of David Brainerd*, (Chicago: Moody Press, 1949), 156-157.

against you." David desired to overcome sin and overcome the wickedness of those conspiring against the ways of the Lord. In Psalm 119:23, he adds, "Even though princes sit plotting against me, your servant will meditate on your statutes." One other example comes from the cherished Psalm 1, where the truly blessed man is he who meditates on the law of God "day and night." He illustratively is like "a tree planted by streams of water that yields its fruit in its season, and its leaf does not whither" (Psalm 1:3).

One beloved divine who wrote prolifically and who specifically wrote a collection of short reflections on biblically discerned concepts and applications was Richard Sibbs, who was at times referred to as "the heavenly Dr. Sibbs" and "The Sweet Dropper." Brother Sibbs was a revered preacher at Cambridge, England (1610-1635, Holy Trinity Church, Cambridge). He wrote many themes and that would be illustrative of the initial thesis of the Puritan effort to strategize in the opposing of the temptations of the flesh, the enticements of the world, and the schemes of the devil.

A few examples of Sibbs from his "Divine Meditations and Holy Contemplations," #25: "Our desires are holy if they be exercised about spiritual things..." This is a reflection upon biblical truth that helps the believer to progress in the journey of sanctification. #40: "Take heed of Satan's policy, that God hath forgotten me..." Such meditation upon biblical truth helps us to not be pushed around by the strategies of spiritual darkness. Another reflection from the more theological concept is a Christological theme from #75: "Christ is our pattern, whom we must strive to imitate..."[50] Not much is written in our modern days preserving the biblical injunction to meditate on the Scriptures. The call to a biblical meditation thus appears greatly diminished since the times of the Puritan writers. From these earlier days of biblically saturated writings of godly men and

---

[50]Richard Sibbs, *Works of Richard Sibbs*: Volume 7 (England: Banner of Truth, 1973), 185-228.

women, the Christian soul must today be nurtured continually through a soul-felt thirsting for the things of God.

The edification of the inner man through Godward contemplation is the pattern prescribed by the Word of God. The Puritans were Christian leaders who championed the right and the fortifying habit of biblical meditation. From a well-crafted book by Joel Beeke called *Reformed Puritan Spirituality* are a few examples from a list of the benefits of biblical meditation by the Puritan pastor, William Bridge. Bridge advocates:

A. Meditation helps us to hear and read the Word with real benefit. It makes the Word "full of life and energy to our souls." William Bates wrote, 'Hearing the Word is like ingestion, and when we meditate upon the word that is digestion; and this digestion of the word by meditation produceth warm affections, zealous resolutions, and holy actions.

B. Meditation stresses the heinousness of sin. It 'musters up all weapons, and gathers all forces of arguments for to press our sins, and lay them upon the heart,' wrote William Fenner.

C. Meditation is a mighty weapon to ward off Satan and temptation (Ps. 119:11, 15; 1 Jn. 2:14).

D. Meditation provides relief in afflictions (Is. 49:15-17; Heb. 12:5).

E. Meditation helps us benefit others with our spiritual fellowship and counsel (Ps. 66:16; 77:12; 145:7).

F. Meditation helps prevent vain and sinful thoughts (Jer. 4:14; Matt. 12:35) It helps wean us from this present evil age.[51]

---

[51]Joel Beeke, *Puritan Reformed Spirituality*, (Grand Rapids: Reformation Heritage Books, 2004), 92-94.

The Outward Assertion of Faith in Worship
and the Declaration of the Gospel Message

The counterpart to the transforming and spiritual protective work of the gospel on the inner man is the outward assertion of faith in both the worship of Almighty God and the declaration of the Kingdom message of Jesus Christ.

From the pen of one modern-day Puritan on the theme touching both worship and the advancement of the gospel through world missions is found in these words, "Missions is not the ultimate goal of the church, worship is. Missions exist because worship doesn't, worship is ultimate, not missions because God is ultimate, not man..."[52] Worship may be practically described as the outward expression of the soul toward God. Literally, worship means in some connotations, "to bow down, to prostrate oneself." One Bible dictionary states, "Homage rendered to God which it is sinful (idolatry) to render to any created being (Ex. 34:14; Isa. 2:8). Such worship was refused by Peter (Acts 10:25-26) and by an angel (Rev. 22:8-9)."[53]

The Scriptures set before us great contexts of the consummation of worship with the people of God in holiness. The psalmist describes the expansiveness of worship in Psalm 22:25-31, describing congregational worship, international worship, and future generations that will yet worship:

From you comes my praise in the great congregation; my vows I will perform before those who fear him. The afflicted shall eat and be satisfied; those who seek him shall praise the LORD! May your hearts live forever! All the ends of the earth shall remember

---

[52]John Piper, *Let the nations be glad*, (Grand Rapids: Baker Academic, 2010), 17.

[53]*Easton's Bible Dictionary*, (e-sword, Public Domain), "worship."

and turn to the LORD, and all the families of the nations shall worship before you. For kingship belongs to the LORD, and he rules over the nations. All the prosperous of the earth eat and worship; before him shall bow all who go down to the dust, even the one who could not keep himself alive. Posterity shall serve him; it shall be told of the Lord to the coming generation; they shall come and proclaim his righteousness to a people yet unborn, that he has done it (Ps. 22:25-31).

The churches stemming from the Reformation differed in the post-Reformation period of the Puritans, from strictly the psalms to the Lutherans who generally held that if something was not forbidden in the Word of God it was permissible in worship. Nevertheless, with voice and heart our worship in song is expressed with the intent to magnify the Triune God. One of the most recognized hymn writers of that era is Isaac Watts (1674-1748). He wrote such well-known hymns from the beloved, "Joy to the World" to the sober, "When I Survey the Wondrous Cross." As well he wrote hymns that bear witness to the themes brought forth in *Battle Cry*, such as "Am I a Soldier of the Cross." The robust lyrics read:

"Am I a soldier of the Cross—
A follower of the Lamb?
And shall I fear to own His cause,
Or blush to speak His name?

In the name, the precious name,
Of Him who died for me,
Through grace I'll win the promised crown,
Whate'er my cross may be.

Must I be carried to the skies
On flowery beds of ease,
While others fought to win the prize
And sailed through bloody seas?

Are there no foes for me to face?
Must I not stem the flood?
Is this vile world a friend to grace,
To help me on to God?

Since I must fight if I would reign,
Increase my courage, Lord!
I'll bear the toil, endure the pain,
Supported by Thy Word."[54]

As well, other expressions of voice and heart accompany the variety of forms of public worship beginning in the earliest days of the church, the era of the post-Reformation church of the Puritans up through modern times. Whether the public reading of Scripture, ministry of song, public corporate praying and joint reading, or reciting the ancient creeds and confessions of the faith, many take part in the outward assertion of faith. From the most remote ventures to bring the gospel to the world, the message of Christ crucified has gone out that worship may be cultivated in the hearts of men, women, and children everywhere. From the days of the Great Commission (Matt. 28:19-20) by the Lord Jesus till today, the good news for mankind has gone out in various ways, from being whispered, taught and to being proclaimed throughout the world. The declaration of the gospel was integral to the Puritan era preaching and life as well.

In the concise book on Puritan evangelism, Beeke explains that one of the primary means of evangelism in the Puritan era was the plain preaching of the Bible in a sermon that was "exegetical," "doctrinal and didactic," and "applicatory."[55] Beeke sets

---

[54] Isaac Watts, *Am I a soldier of the Cross*, (Public Domain, 1721).

[55] Joel Beeke, *Puritan Evangelism: A Biblical Approach*, (Grand Rapids: reformation Heritage Books, 2007).

forth three characteristics that marked the plain preaching of Puritan messengers:

1) "Puritan Preaching addressed the Mind with Clarity," 2) "Puritan preaching confronted the conscience pointedly," and 3) "Puritan preaching wooed the heart passionately."[56]

In defining the fullness of the gospel that was traditional Puritan evangelistic, Beeke states (their messages often involved), "...declaring the entire economy of redemption by focusing on the saving work of all three persons of the Trinity while simultaneously calling sinners to a life of faith and commitment; and warning that the gospel will condemn forever those who persist in unbelief and impenitence."[57]

One Puritan preacher well known for his persistent preaching and passionate devotion to the cross-centered life was John Bunyan. In his classic writing, *The Pilgrim's Progress*, the character Evangelist appears at precise points in the journey of the pilgrim named Christian. Early on in the account of the story of Christian, the following situation occurred, "Now one day when he was walking in the fields..."[58]

The man in the story appears to Christian just at the time in which Christian is lost, confused, and burdened by sin; he is able to point Christian to a very helpful landmark called "the wicket gate," and to another landmark called "a shining light." Being told the direction to go and the urgent instruction to "flee the wrath to come," Christian went on his way.

---

[56] Ibid, 59-61.
[57] Ibid, 6.
[58] John Bunyan, *The Pilgrims Progress*, (Project Gutenberg. Public Domain), https://www.gutenberg.org/files/39452/39452-h/39452-h.htm, 2-3.

The era of the Puritans contributes much to the church of the Millennial generation, and much that can be lost if it is not cherished and studied by present and future saints. Countless Puritan literary treasures are in circulation today, yet remain for much of the body of Christ as untapped treasures, unopened and of tremendous spiritual value. In closing, consider the thoughts of Thomas Watson in the classic book entitled, *The Godly Man's Picture*. Watson writes, "Walking in the ways of sin is like walking of the banks of a river. The sinner treads on the banks..." [59]

Questions for Spiritual Formation:

1. What are some tangible ways that the saint must resolve to pursue and be compelled by God to move toward this spoken of "inner fortification of transforming grace"?

2. Considering the divine ordinance of the Lord's Supper. How is this "knowledge and righteous test of one's conscience the path to right examination when we arrive at the Lord's Table?"

3. Review the idea of an "outward assertion of faith in an advancement of the Kingdom message of Christ crucified." What forms does this take in the believer's life?

4. In what ways are the Puritans today a time-tested era of history that the Christian should acquire spiritual enrichment from?

---

[59] Thomas Watson, *The Godly Man's Picture*, (Carlisle: Banner of Truth, 1992), 180.

May God bestow on us His grace
by Martin Luther

May God bestow on us His grace,
With blessings rich provide us,
And may the brightness of His face
To life eternal guide us
That we His saving health may know,
His gracious will and pleasure,
And also to the heathen show
Christ's riches without measure
And unto God convert them.
Thine over all shall be the praise
And thanks of every nation,
And all the world with joy shall raise
The voice of exultation;
For Thou shalt judge the earth, O Lord,
Nor suffer sin to flourish;
Thy people's pasture is Thy Word
Their souls to feed and nourish,
In righteous paths to keep them.
Oh, let the people praise Thy worth,
In all good works increasing;
The land shall plenteous fruit bring forth,
Thy Word is rich in blessing,
May God the Father, God the Son,
And God the Spirit bless us!
Let all the world praise Him alone,
Let solemn awe possess us,
Now let our hearts say, Amen.[60]

---

[60]Martin Luther, *May God Bestow on us His Grace*, (Public Domain, 1524).

Characteristics of the Cross-Centered Combatant

Chapter 6

The Gospel Warrior as Ambassador

In April of 1915 tens of thousands of Armenian men were rounded up and shot. Hundreds of thousands of women, old men, and children were deported south across the mountains to Cilicia and Syria. On April 15 the Armenians appealed to the German Ambassador in Constantinople for formal German protection. This was rejected by Berlin on the grounds that it would offend the Turkish Government. By April 19 more than 50,000 Armenians had been murdered in the Van province.

Within nine months, more than 600,000 Armenians were massacred. Of the deported during that same period, more than 400,000 perished of the brutalities and privations of the southward march into Mesopotamia. By September more than a million Armenians were the victims of what later became known as the Armenian Genocide! A further 200,000 were forcibly converted to Islam to give Armenia a new Turkish sense of identity and strip the Armenian people of their past as the first Christian state in the world.[61]

Ambassador Morgenthau's Story became one of the most insightful and compelling accounts of what became a recurring horror during the 20th century: ethnic cleansing and genocide. While he served as the U.S. ambassador to the Ottoman Empire under Woodrow Wilson from 1913 to 1916, Henry

---

[61]Genocide 1915, "Armenian Genocide Timeline:1917," http://www.genocide1915.info/history/1917/.

Morgenthau witnessed the rise of a new nationalism in Turkey, one that declared 'Turkey for the Turks.' He grew alarmed as he received reports from missionaries and consuls in the interior of Turkey that described deportation and massacre of the Armenians. The ambassador beseeched the U.S. government to intervene, but it refrained, leaving Morgenthau without official leverage....

Average citizens in the United States came to the aid of Armenians. The first international aid mission of the American Red Cross was to help Armenian victims of the 1896 massacres. In 1915, the American Committee for Armenian and Syrian Relief was established, raising millions of dollars to save the 'starving Armenians,' a term in common use at the time. Chartered by the U.S. Congress in 1919 as Near East Relief, it established refugee camps, hospitals, and orphanages, delivering food, clothing, shelter materials, and providing genocide survivors with job training.

Overall, the Near East Relief cared for 132,000 Armenian orphans scattered across the region...In May 1915, the Allies characterized the extermination of the Armenians as a "crime against humanity..." Because the perpetrators were not punished and no restitution was made to the victims, Adolf Hitler saw it as a valid precedent for his plan to wipe out the Jews of Europe. In a speech before invading Poland in 1939, Hitler spoke proudly of his intention to kill "mercilessly," saying, "Who, after all, speaks today of the annihilation of the Armenians?"[62]

[62]The Genocide Education Project, The Armenian Genocide, https://genocideeducation.org/background/brief-history/.

President Woodrow Wilson urged former ambassador Henry Morgenthau to write a book based on his experiences.[63] *Ambassador Morgenthau's Story* (1918) the printed memoirs of Henry Morgenthau, Sr. (U.S. Ambassador to the Ottoman Empire from 1913 to 1916). The volume was dedicated to Woodrow Wilson (the serving U.S. President at the time). The book is a primary source regarding the Armenian Genocide (taking two years to its completion). The writing included the account of the massacre of the Greeks as well.

The commissioned U.S. ambassador to Turkey, Morgenthau went to do what was asked of him and report to the U.S. president. Likewise, the Christ-follower today is an ambassador of a heavenly message, entrusted with the eternal message of the gospel, and commissioned to represent heaven and the God who has entrusted them with the responsibility of a gospel ambassador.

> All this is from God, who through Christ reconciled us to himself and gave us the ministry of reconciliation; that is, in Christ God was reconciling the world to himself, not counting their trespasses against them, and entrusting to us the message of reconciliation. Therefore, we are *ambassadors* for Christ, God making his appeal through us. We implore you on behalf of Christ, be reconciled to God. For our sake he made him to be sin who knew no sin, so that in him we might become the righteousness of God (2 Cor. 5:18-21, emphasis added).

In 2 Corinthians, the apostle Paul was writing to the Corinthian Church in roughly late AD 56. His message and the main purposes in writing was to help the Corinthian Church to go further in their faith and pursuit of God. There were a few reasons for the letter.

---

[63] Genocide 1915, Armenian Genocide.

One reason was to communicate his great confidence in God through all the suffering and persecution he endured. Second, to reinforce that God had indeed called him and bestowed upon him the genuine office of an apostle, as he had been attacked and accused of inauthenticity. (In reality he was not promoting himself, but the greater certainty of the Kingdom purposes of God, and the gospel message of the Kingdom.) Third, Paul was writing to express his great joy in hearing that the Corinthian believers responded well to the correction/instruction he gave to them as an apostle of Jesus Christ. Furthermore, he was writing perhaps concerning lesser matters as well or arguably other more important issues. In 2 Corinthians Paul discloses his heart and life in a distinct way compared to much of his other writing.

This chapter is concerned about another component of 2 Corinthians 5:20: "The ministry of reconciliation." The focus will be in two points: 1) the messenger (considering here matters about the divine role of the messenger); and 2) the meat of the message (the divine news entrusted and represented).

The Messenger

Notice that Paul begins the verse with a ministry statement (foremost here of Paul's apostolic ministry): "Therefore we are ambassadors for Christ." Paul is referring to himself here (and the pronoun *we*, definitely includes other ministers of the gospel, i.e., Paul's missionary companions). The apostles generally may be referred to here, and to all who have a part in the spiritual leadership of carrying the message of Christ, as messengers of the gospel. An *ambassador* is usually understood as an individual of rank sent by a government to represent it, conduct its business with the government officials of another country.

One basic identity of an ambassador is to represent the sending government to deliver its words. Another Bible dictionary states that "the Hebrews on various occasions and for various purposes used the service of ambassadors" (e.g., to contract alliances, to solicit political favors, to bring confrontation when wrong was done, and to congratulate a king who was inaugurated in ascending a throne or rulership). If someone were to injure an ambassador it would be an insult to the king that sent him.

In the Old Testament, 2 Samuel, King David sent ambassadors to represent himself, to bring consolation to the son of the king of the Ammonites (after the king of the Ammonites died). In carrying the message of King David, the messengers that went as representatives were accused of being spies, the people reacted violently towards them, shaved off half their beards, cut their garments down to their hips, and sent them away. This would have been an extreme insult to King David personally.

In another very illustrative depiction, the apostle Paul uses the very same word in Ephesians 6:19-20 that he used in 2 Corinthians 5:20. He states, "and also for me, that words may be given to me in opening my mouth boldly to proclaim the mystery of the gospel, for which I am an *ambassador in chains*, that I may declare it boldly, as I ought to speak" (Eph. 6:19-20, emphasis added). He was indeed an ambassador of God, carrying the precious message of heaven. Here the imagery is of a striking contrast of an *ambassador in chains* (i.e., normally ambassadors would not be expected to be seen in chains).

It should be emphasized that he was indeed imprisoned for the gospel while he wrote the epistles. It is well respected that Paul wrote during his imprisonment of AD 62-64. Moreover, it is certainly significant that Paul uses the terminology of an ambassador. One Bible commentator writes:

He was an ambassador- sent to proclaim peace to a lost world. But he was now in chains. An ambassador is a sacred character. No greater affront can be given to a nation than to put its ambassadors to death, or even to throw them into prison. But Paul says here that the unusual spectacle was witnessed of an ambassador seized, bound, confined, imprisoned; an ambassador who ought to have the privileges

86

conceded to all such people, and to be permitted to go every-where publishing the terms of mercy and salvation.[64]

We can add that an ambassador should have free access to the hearing and hearts of the people. He represented heaven and the Kingdom of God. Yet he was treated poorly as many of the Old Testament prophets were.

In the main text of this chapter (2 Cor. 5:20), we are considering the divine messenger and that Paul and his missionary companions were ambassadors of the gospel. Let us not forget that believers today—who understand the Great Commission of Jesus—are spiritual ambassadors. The term *ambassador* here is not a technical term, it can be applied to every messenger of the gospel of Jesus Christ. The wording "for Christ" again emphasizing the sending agent, the country of origin that sent the ambassador to convey its message, and it has the sense that Paul and his missionary companions were representatives of the gospel, on behalf of Christ. The relationship then of the gospel messenger is that he goes in the place of Jesus, representing Him and he goes for the sake of His cause.

It is of the utmost importance here to see that Paul, his missionary traveling companions, the other apostles, and all who carry the message of the gospel of Jesus Christ are ambassadors for the sake of Jesus. Here we see a little more of the heart of the apostle Paul, who exhorts believers to follow him as he followed Jesus Christ. Additionally, Paul has laid down his life for the cause of Christ. One Expositors Bible Commentary expresses here that for Paul, "The fire that burned in Christ's heart has caught hold of his...as Christ's ambassador and as the mouthpiece for God, in his humility, in his passionate earnestness, in the urgency and directness of his appeal, St. Paul is the supreme type and example of the Christian minister."[65]

---

[64] Albert Barnes, *Barnes notes on the Bible*, (Public Domain, 1847-85).
[65] *Expositors Bible Commentary* (Public Domain, 1887-1896).

Indeed, Paul was modeling the love of Christ that lays down one's life for his friends in his circumstance of being an ambassador in chains. The believer today may reflect on their own lives with questions like, "Has that fire caught hold of my heart that had caught hold of the heart of the apostle Paul?" and "Have I sensed that great 'passionate earnestness'?"

The Meat of the Message
(The Divine News)

"God making his appeal through us. We implore you on behalf of Christ, be reconciled to God" (2 Cor. 5:20).

Here, I urge you to consider the content or the meat of the divine message, this good news that the ambassador has the privilege to deliver to his or her recipients.

The wording of this verse, "God making his appeal through us" gives the sense that God is the One calling through the messenger. Being an ambassador for Christ is the same as if God is making an appeal through us. In 5:19, Paul says God has committed to the messenger "the message of reconciliation". However, it is just as if it were God making His appeal. As Paul states, "we implore you on behalf of Christ, be reconciled to God."

In the divine character of the message, both God the Father and God the Son are included in describing the heavenly content of the message. It is as if God were making an appeal through us. The gospel messenger is therefore an ambassador for Christ. Again, the message is given as though God Himself were giving it through the messenger and it is in Christ's place the message is delivered.

So, in light of this Christ-centered/God-centered context, the apostle Paul begs us to be reconciled to God. The wording here is very much an urgent request, an imploring and a begging. It is certainly characteristic of Paul to present the gospel in this urgent sense, entreating people and pleading with people. This specific type of gospel begging here presents Paul as a pleader or one who implores people. He eagerly desires for everyone and anyone to hear the truth of God, to call out to anyone who will listen. The word Paul uses—*beg*, or *entreat* or *implore*—he uses in the other epistles that he wrote, and New Testament verses where he is quoted.

One example where Paul also uses the same expression is in Galatians 4:12, where he says, "Brothers, I entreat you, become as I am." He was calling to Jewish believers in Galatia to repent of bringing legalism with them from their Jewish background. Paul is also quoted in Acts 21:39 where he pleads with the Romans for a hearing, "Paul replied, 'I am a Jew, from Tarsus in Cilicia, a citizen of no obscure city. I *beg* you, permit me to speak to the people'" (emphasis added). As well, here's a verse where Paul is speaking before the pagan King Agrippa: "I beg you to listen to me patiently" (Acts 26:3). Second Corinthians 10:2 shows Paul pleading, "I beg of you." Paul is absolutely known as a pleader in this way, for the purposes of God, a beggar to the people of God to hear his cause and what he wanted so much to communicate to them.

We can benefit here from the apostolic passion of Paul. So, in this begging, pleading to be heard for the sake of the eternal souls of the listeners, Paul says, "Be reconciled to God," or as the old KJV expresses it, "Be ye reconciled to God." That was the meat of the message, as it were. Paul and all gospel ambassadors bring this challenge to every soul. Primarily, the idea is that before it is too late, you must be born again (John 3:3), or again "be ye reconciled to God." It is noteworthy this phrase contains an imperative verb here. It signifies to do something urgently, do this thing now. And perhaps the most wonderful thing about the verb is that it is a passive verb, it also signifies something that one emphatically does not have the power to do, rather it is something that God does for you.

The biblical posture for the man or woman of God here is that of absolute surrender to God. Subsequently, the right message that the ambassador of Christ is to give out is the same call to surrender. It is the total acceptance of the reconciliation that has been provided for us on the cross: "that is, in Christ God was reconciling the world to himself, not counting their trespasses against them, and entrusting to us the message of reconciliation. Therefore, we are ambassadors for Christ, with God making his appeal through us. We implore you on behalf of Christ, be reconciled to God" (2 Cor. 5:19-20). Just as Paul implores his readers, I encourage you to declare the tireless treasure of the truth of the gospel to all, and particularly to those who need it most.

Questions for Spiritual Formation:

1. Why is the Pauline auto-biographical description of an "ambassador in chains" a profound illustration of the life of Paul?

2. Why does the name "spiritual ambassador" fit well even the modern missionary today?

3. Considering the Great Commission (Matt. 28:19-20), why is the message so urgent that it is fair to say that every Christian is a form of this spiritual ambassador?

4. In what ways can we strive to communicate from our hearts the message that requires us to plead with lost souls about this crucial need to be reconciled with God?

We've a Story to Tell to the Nations
By H. Ernest Nichol

We've a story to tell to the nations,
that shall turn their hearts to the right,
a story of truth and mercy,
a story of peace and light,
a story of peace and light.

Refrain:
For the darkness shall turn to dawning,
and the dawning to noonday bright;
and Christ's great kingdom shall come on earth,
the kingdom of love and light.

We've a song to be sung to the nations,
that shall lift their hearts to the Lord,
a song that shall conquer evil
and shatter the spear and sword,
and shatter the spear and sword.

We've a message to give to the nations,
that the Lord who reigneth above
hath sent us his Son to save us,
and show us that God is love,
and show us that God is love.

We've a Savior to show to the nations,
who the path of sorrow hath trod,
that all of the world's great peoples
might come to the truth of God,
might come to the truth of God.[66]

---

[66]H. Ernest Nichol, *We've a Story to Tell to the Nations* (Public Domain, 1896).

Chapter 7   # The Gospel Warrior as Soldier

"Jocko Willink, a former U.S. Navy SEAL went into his retirement after 20 years with the teams in 2010. Willink commanded the renowned unit, Task Unit Bruiser, the special forces element with the most military honors during the war in Iraq. He has shared his continual rigorous work-out routine that he maintains in the years after his career with the SEALS. From a recent interview, Willink shares how a typical day begins:

1. Wake up at 4:30 a.m. Three alarms are set — one electric, one battery-powered, and one windup — but he almost always only needs one. The two others are safeguards.

2. After a quick cleanup in the bathroom, take a photo of wristwatch to show his Twitter followers what time he's beginning the day. It's become both a way to hold himself accountable as well as inspire others to stick to their goals.

3. Grab his workout clothes, laid out the night before, and head to the gym in his garage for one of the following strength workouts, which lasts around an hour. The exercises can either be lower weight with high reps and little rest or heavy weight with low reps and lots of rest.

   • Day 1: Pull ups, muscle ups, related exercises.

- Day 2: Overhead lifts, bench press, deadlifts, handstand push-ups, kettle-bell swings.
- Day 3: Ring dips, regular dips, push-ups.
- Day 4: Overhead squats, front squats, regular squats.

4. Spend anywhere from a few minutes (intense bursts) to a half hour (steady) for cardiovascular training. This could include sprints or a jog.

5. Finish workout around 6:00 a.m. Depending on the day, go out to hit the beach near his home near San Diego, California, to spend time swimming or surfing. If the weather is nice, he may also do his cardio on the beach.

6. Shower and start working for his leadership consulting firm, Echelon Front, any time after 6:00 a.m. He doesn't get hungry until around noon, and only has a snack, like a few handfuls of nuts, in the morning.

7. After work, Willink gets in two hours of jiu-jitsu training and heads to bed around 11:00 pm.

Willink said that he recognizes that everyone is different, and that not everyone would benefit from getting up at 4:00 a.m. for an intense workout. The key is that 'you get up and move,' whether that's jogging, weight lifting, or yoga. The discipline comes in setting a schedule and sticking to it so that your day begins with an energizing accomplishment, not a demoralizing stretch of time where you lie in bed and hit snooze on your alarm a few times. Every morning should start off with a predictable routine."[67]

---

[67]Richard Feloni, A retired Navy SEAL commander breaks down his morning fitness routine that starts before dawn, *Business Insider*. http://www.businessinsider.com/retired-navy-seal-jocko-willinks-morning-routine-2015-11.

This routine describes a rigorous discipline that would require strict goals and purposes in one's life. Certainly, much more can be accomplished for the Kingdom of God when one utilizes the God-given minutes and hours that make up every day, that do not allow for habits of laziness and indiscipline to creep in. The apostle Paul expresses many similar sentiments as this, as he desired to honor the Lord with his time, energy, and goals. Paul states such a strict concentration was needed, thus, "making the best use of the time, because the days are evil" (Eph. 5:16).

Paul taught the disciplined stewardship of time, body, energy, and resources, and he also applied this type of focus—a militarily disciplined life—for the purpose of pleasing his supervisor or higher ranking soldier or officer, as he states "the one who enlisted him" (2 Tim. 2:4). Paul carries the metaphor of the disciplined soldier to the biblically minded and spiritually disciplined Christian soldier. Paul wrote to exhort Timothy, the church elder and missionary partner that he was grooming for further leadership ability:

And what you have heard from me in the presence of many witnesses entrust to faithful men, who will be able to teach others also. Share in suffering as a good soldier of Christ Jesus. No soldier gets entangled in civilian pursuits, since his aim is to please the one who enlisted him (2 Tim. 2:2-4).

The analogy of a soldier here can hardly be overlooked when considering the larger theme of 2 Timothy. The picture of the diligent and disciplined combatant captures much meaning here to include application to both the full-time vocational minister and the individual Christ follower, both of whom must look to the imagery of soldier. The believer is to live in a focused and dedicated stance that depicts the same concentration as the soldier committed to maintaining his role and fighting position in a battlefield environment.

The backdrop of the text at hand is the apostle Paul writing in chains while imprisoned for the cause of the gospel. Here he writes initially to Timothy—his son in the faith, missionary traveling partner, and the preaching elder of the church in the city of Ephesus. He is charging Timothy to heartily take up the cause of the gospel with the tenacity and discipline of a soldier that is prepared and dedicated to his combat-focused requirements. Paul charges Timothy with a military-type commission in 2 Timothy 2-4, which include:

1. The mission: training others for the battle
2. The conditions: sharing in the sufferings of the calling
3. The battlefield mindset: focus on warrior vocation (not civilian distractions).

The Mission: Training Others for the Battle

"And what you have heard from me in the presence of many witnesses entrust to faithful men, who will be able to teach others also" (2 Tim. 2:2).

Regarding the mission at hand, in the context of 2 Timothy 2:2-4, it is found that a man of God must be diligent about preparing the next team of gospel soldiers for the work of the Christian life. The mission is the training of disciples who are then able to train others. It is the mission of the guardian/warrior to pass on the entrusted treasure to those that will come after him or her, whose lives will outlast his or her own.

The treasure keeper of the gospel must have this mindset to always be about preparing others for the fight, to always have ready other capable and spiritually gifted leaders. The English Baptist pastor, John Gill, wrote about this responsibility:

> ... to faithful men; who not only have received the grace of God, and are true believers in Christ, but are men of great uprightness and integrity; who having the word of God, will speak it out boldly, and faithfully, and keep back nothing that

is profitable, but declare the whole counsel of God, without any mixture or adulteration; for the Gospel being committed to their trust, they would become stewards, and of such it is required that they be faithful; and therefore this is mentioned as a necessary and requisite qualification in them.[68]

In the discipline of military training, the mentorship of young, new soldiers is an enormous task, one that is inherent to the work of the soldier. The tragedy of never having a replacement should not occur; if one man goes down on the field of battle, another should be fully prepared to take his place on the line of defense. This truth of having ready replacements in the battle is definitely relevant to the subsequent portion of the life of a soldier.

The Conditions: Sharing in the Sufferings of the Calling

As a title, this may sound overdramatically descriptive. However, the heaven-sent stewardship of the message of Christ is to be faithfully upheld and proclaimed both in times of suffering, adversity, and times of peace. The goal is to glorify God through seeing lives changed by the heavenly words, but as Paul instructs, this may include the role of suffering if the situation demands it be so. This is not what the Christian necessarily looks forward to in any way. The gospel of "easy-believism" definitely will shy away from verses like this, yet it is analogous to the life of the true disciple or the authentic Christian that Paul exhorts Timothy to.

Paul's mandate for the gospel soldier here is admittedly unnerving, it is literally "to suffer hardship," to endure afflictions in the Christian life. The Christian walk is paralleled to the rigorous discipline of a soldier or warrior. Calvin, thus states:

---

[68]John Gill, *Gill's Exposition of the Bible*, (Public Domain, 1816).

...without patient endurance of evils, there will never be perseverance. And accordingly he adds, 'as becomes a *good soldier of Jesus Christ.*' By this term he means that all who serve Christ are warriors, and that their condition as warriors consists, not in inflicting evils, but rather in patience.[69]

If the illustrative comparison here is a soldier, in the like manner that a soldier perseveres in hardship, so the genuine disciple should never expect less. A soldier may by necessity endure under the pressure of austere conditions. It may be obligatory for the soldier to undergo enemy fire, at the mercy of the elements (be it cold, snow, rain, hail, wind, or heat). Military personnel are trained to endure extreme adversity under circumstances of fatigue, hunger, thirst, pressures of evasion of the enemy, or even the conditions that prisoners of war faced.

At times in history, U.S. troops have fought extraordinarily in adversity, yet extensive documentation is available today to study, and understand inspirationally the extent to which our soldiers "endured hardship." One of the most atrocious battles of WWII, the beginning of the end of the war, is known as the Battle of the Bulge (the events surrounding 16 Dec. 1944). As it appeared that the Allies could pursue an end of the war, General Eisenhower supported the advance of over 500,000 personnel into the battle. The conditions there were horrid, according to historians:

> The soldiers often fought in zero-temperature conditions and driving snow that prevented them from seeing more than 10 or 20 yards in front of them. With equipment and uniforms that were designed for warmer times, frostbite became a terrible reality. Because soldiers were often cut off from their

---

[69]John Calvin, *Commentaries on The Epistles to Timothy, Titus, and Philemon*, (Grand Rapids: Baker Book House, 1998), 210.

divisions in foxholes, the wounded, in some cases, literally froze to death.[70]

As Allied soldiers waged war against the evil forces of Nazism, so Christian leaders and fundamentally all Christians are called to consider the call to engage the battle as soldiers of the cross. Suffering hardship or "be thou partaker of the afflictions" (2 Tim. 1:8, KJV) as a common characteristic of the Christian life is found as Paul exhorts Timothy in 2 Timothy 1:8: "Therefore do not be ashamed of the testimony about our Lord, nor of me his prisoner, but share in suffering for the gospel by the power of God."

The apostle Paul, writing as a veteran warrior for Christ, was communicating to Timothy, a junior soldier to Paul. The simile of a soldier is used often to describe the Christian life. (Paul uses military figures of speech with frequency in his writings, as in Romans 7:23; 1 Corinthians 9:7; 2 Corinthians 6:7; Ephesians 6:11-18.) Again the climate of the warfare described is that which would involve suffering. Though addressed initially to Timothy, suffering or affliction related to living the Christian life in this present world is consistent with Scripture. In distinguishing between suffering for the cause of Christ versus suffering for some other type of cause, Pastor/teacher John MacArthur has written:

> It is important to note that Paul is speaking about suffering for the gospel, not about suffering punishment for our sinfulness. But when we live a godly, moral life before our family, our fellow students, our fellow workers, or our neighbors, we can expect hostility in some form or another because their immorality or ungodliness will be more apparent by contrast.[71]

---

[70]Alcee L. Hastings, Recognizing the 60th Anniversary of the Battle of the Bulge During World War II, Congressional Record online through the Government Publishing Office.

[71]John MacArthur, *The MacArthur New Testament Commentaries 2 Timothy* (Chicago: The Moody Bible Insttute, 1995), 21.

Paul goes on to instruct Timothy of the wider application for all believers: "Indeed, all who desire to live a godly life in Christ Jesus will be persecuted" (2 Tim. 3:12). (Also see John 16:33; 2 Cor. 6:4-7; Acts 5:41.)

The Battlefield Mindset:
Focus on Warrior Vocation
(not civilian distractions)

The spiritual warfare mindset is explicit in 2 Timothy 2: 2-4; in other words, the apostle Paul is speaking plainly and directly. The standard called for by the holy apostle is to absolutely distinguish between the disciplined focus like that of a combat-trained soldier and that of another individual who is a civilian and who has totally different priorities in life. The soldier here in the context is on active duty and has the continual constraints of his vocation calling him to recall his commitment to the people, place, or nation he is defending. For example, some type of training mission or actual combat operation would be required of him at some point, and would undeniably demand his undivided attention. He cannot allow himself to be distracted by the activities, thoughts, or conduct that would be inconsistent with what he has been commanded to do. Calvin expresses further that Paul:

> ...continues to make use of the metaphor which he had borrowed from warfare. Yet, strictly speaking, he formerly called Timothy "a soldier of Christ" metaphorically; but now he compares profane warfare with spiritual and Christian warfare in this sense. "The condition of military discipline is such, that as soon as a soldier has enrolled himself under a general, he leaves his house and all his affairs, and thinks of nothing but war; and in like manner, in order that we may be

wholly devoted to Christ, we must be free from all the entanglements of this world.[72]

This aspect of the Christian life and ministry is both strategic and something that requires discernment. Many have gone to extremes (for example, ancient monasticism that developed into an isolationist- and at times solitary way of life in Roman Catholic monasteries and convents). Those that have committed themselves to lives of physical separation and have forgotten that the fight of the Christian life is in the trenches of the human society in which we live.

Questions for Spiritual Formation:

1. Though often taught separately, how can 2 Timothy 2:2—"and what you have heard from me in the presence of many witnesses entrust to faithful men, who will be able to teach others also"—be practically applied to the life of a soldier of the cross?

2. How is the life Paul was exhorting Timothy to follow, and the standard for all Christians, like that of a soldier, as in: "Share in suffering as a good soldier of Christ Jesus" (2 Tim. 2:3)?

3. From 2 Timothy 2:4— "No soldier gets entangled in civilian pursuits, since his aim is to please the one who enlisted him"—what is distinctive to a military life that helps us to see what Paul was compelling Timothy to embrace?

---

[72]Calvin, *Timothy, Titus, and Philemon,* 208-211.

Onward, Christian soldiers
By Sabine Baring-Gould

Onward, Christian soldiers, marching as to war,
With the cross of Jesus going on before.
Christ, the royal Master, leads against the foe;
Forward into battle see His banners go!

Refrain:
Onward, Christian soldiers, marching as to war,
With the cross of Jesus going on before.

At the sign of triumph Satan's host doth flee;
On then, Christian soldiers, on to victory!
Hell's foundations quiver at the shout of praise;
Brothers lift your voices, loud your anthems raise.

Like a mighty army moves the church of God;
Brothers, we are treading where the saints have trod.
We are not divided, all one body we,
One in hope and doctrine, one in charity.

Crowns and thrones may perish, kingdoms rise and wane,
But the church of Jesus constant will remain.
Gates of hell can never gainst that church prevail;
We have Christ's own promise, and that cannot fail.

Onward then, ye people, join our happy throng,
Blend with ours your voices in the triumph song.
Glory, laud and honor unto Christ the King,
This through countless ages men and angels sing.[73]

---

[73]Sabine Baring-Gould, Onward Christian Soldiers, (Public Domain, 1865).

Chapter 8

The Gospel Warrior as Fisherman

While walking by the Sea of Galilee, he saw two brothers, Simon (who is called Peter) and Andrew his brother, casting a net into the sea, for they were fishermen. And he said to them, 'Follow me, and I will make you fishers of men.' Immediately they left their nets and followed him. And going on from there he saw two other brothers, James the son of Zebedee and John his brother, in the boat with Zebedee their father, mending their nets, and he called them. Immediately they left the boat and their father and followed him (Matt. 4:18-22).

As a reflection upon this wondrous theme of God making men into fishers of men, this chapter leads with observations and thoughts from the Puritan pastor Thomas Boston (1676 –1732).[74] Boston remarks:

---

[74]Christian Classics Ethereal Library, Biography, Thomas Boston, http://www.ccel.org/ccel/boston, "Boston was born at Duns. His father, John Boston, and his mother, Alison Trotter, were both Covenanters. He was educated at Edinburgh, and licensed in 1697 by the presbytery of Chirnside. In 1699 he became minister of the small parish of Simprin, where there were only 90 examinable persons…Boston, if unduly introspective, was a man of singular piety and amiability. His autobiography is an interesting record of Scottish life, full of sincerity and tenderness, and not devoid of humorous touches, intentional and otherwise. His books, *The Fourfold State*, *The Crook in the Lot*, and his *Body of*

How Does Christ Make Men Fishers of Men? In answer to this question, consider spiritual fishing two ways: first, as to the office and work itself; and second, as to the success of it. First, he makes them fishers as to their office, by his call, which is twofold, outward and inward, by setting them apart to the office of the ministry; and it is thy business, O my soul, to know whether thou hast it or not. But of this more afterwards.

Second, he makes them fishers as to success; that is, he makes them catch men to himself by the power of his Spirit accompanying the word they preach, and the discipline they administer: The preaching of the cross — unto us which are saved, is the power of God (1 Cor. 1:18). Our gospel came not unto you in word only, but also in power, and in the Holy Ghost, and in much assurance (1 Thess. 1:5). He it is that brings sinners into the net which ministers spread; and if he be not with them to drive the fish into the net, they may toil all the night, and day too, and catch nothing.
O my soul, then see that gifts will not do the business.

A man may preach as an angel, and yet be useless. If Christ withdraw his presence, all will be to no purpose. If the Master of the house be away, the household will loath their food though it be dropping down about their tent doors. Why shouldst thou then, on the one hand, as sometimes thou art, be lifted up when thou preachest a good and solid discourse, wherein gifts do appear, and thou gettest the applause of men? Why, thou mayst do all this, and yet be no fisher of

---

Divinity and Miscellanies, had a powerful influence over the Scottish peasantry. His *Memoirs* were published in 1776. An edition of his works in 12 volumes appeared in 1849."

men. The fish may see the bait, and play about it as pleasant, but this is not enough to catch them.

On the other hand, why shouldst thou be so much discouraged (as many times is the case), because thy gifts are so small, and thou art but as a child in comparison of others? Why, if Christ will, he can make thee a fisher of men, as well as the most learned rabbi in the church: Out of the mouths of babes and sucklings hast thou ordained strength (Ps. 8:2). Yea, hast thou not observed how God owned a man very weak in gifts and made him more successful than others that were far beyond him in parts? Has not God put this treasure in earthen vessels, that the power might be seen to be of him? Lift up thyself then, O my soul, Christ can make thee a fisher of men, however weak thou art. Follow thou him. My soul desires to follow hard after thee, O God!

Be concerned then, in the first place, O my soul, for the presence of God in ordinances, and for his power that will make a change among people (Ps. 110:3). When thy discourse, though ever so elaborate, shall be but as a lovely song, O set thyself most for this. When thou studiest, send up ejaculations to thy Lord for it. When thou writest a sermon, or dost ruminate on it, then say to God, 'Lord, this will be altogether weak without thy power accompanying it.' O power and life from God in ordinances is sweet. Seek it for thyself, and seek it for thy hearers. Acknowledge thine own weakness and uselessness without it, and so cry incessantly for it, that the Lord may drive the fish into the net, when thou art spreading it out.

Have an eye to this power, when thou art preaching; and think not thou to convert men by the force of reason: if thou do, thou wilt be beguiled. What an honorable thing is it to be fishers of men! How great an honor shouldst thou esteem it, to be a catcher of souls! We are workers together with God, says the apostle. If God has ever so honored thee, O that thou knewest it that thou mightst bless his holy name, that ever made such a poor fool as thee to be a co-worker with him. God has owned thee to do good to those who were before caught. O my soul, bless thou the Lord. Lord, what am I, or what is my father's house, that thou hast brought me to this?

Then seest thou not here what is the reason thou toilest so long, and catchest nothing? The power comes not along. Men are like Samuel, who when God was calling him, thought it had been Eli. So when thou speakest many times, they do not discern God's voice, but thine; and therefore the word goest out as it comes in.[75]

In Matthew's gospel, as in others, when it was time, Jesus went forth proclaiming the Kingdom of God, calling for people to repent of their sins. In the beginning of the gospel accounts are found various details of the calling of the apostles. From Mark's parallel account, "Follow me, and I will make you fishers of men." To Luke's quote of Jesus where He calms their fears saying, "Do not be afraid, from now on you will be catching men." And to include John's account where Andrew and another were walking after Jesus and Jesus asks them what they are looking for in 1:38. They reply with the question, "Where are you staying?" Jesus responds in 1:39, "Come and you will see."

This chapter will unfold by focusing on the clear instruction by the Lord Jesus, first to Peter and Andrew, "Follow me, and I will make you fishers of men." This study can be looked at in two parts: 1) the call of self-abandonment; and 2) the call to others-ness (an eternal focused compassion for others).

---

[75]Thomas Boston, *The Art of Man fishing, A Puritan's View of Evangelism,* (Public Domain, 1773), 8-10.

The Call of Self-Abandonment

Jesus called Peter and Andrew saying, "Follow me." There is nothing else written in reference to the first part of the quote of the Lord to the two fishermen (of the Matthean account). That does not mean that was the extent of the conversation. The intent was a complete self-abandonment of personal agenda, dreams, and aspirations. The apostles modeled for all time that when Jesus calls a man, he calls the man to lay everything aside to pursue the leading of Christ, and to embrace the new life that Jesus calls them to.

The call of Jesus was and is this call of self-abandonment, and it is seen in some of the later usages of the phrase in the gospel accounts. Jesus spoke this way throughout the Gospels. In the passage of true discipleship, exemplified by this relinquishment of self, is the same concept "Then Jesus told his disciples, 'If anyone would come after me, let him deny himself and take up his cross and follow me. For whoever would save his life will lose it, but whoever loses his life for my sake will find it'" (Matt. 16:24-25).

Once more, here is expressed the losing of one's life for the Kingdom of God. As well, in John 12:25-26, "Whoever loves his life loses it, and whoever hates his life in this world will keep it for eternal life. If anyone serves me, he must follow me; and where I am, there will my servant be also. If anyone serves me, the Father will honor him." This text repeats the concept of self-abandonment in the pursuit of Christ.

The call by Christ was, in the case of the apostles, and is, in the case of every believer, a call to the relinquishing of self-centeredness for the glory of God and His Kingdom purposes. Come follow Him and lay up your treasure in heaven. In the book, *Follow Me: A Call to Die, A Call to Live*, author David Platt writes of an account about a real woman named Ayan stating:

Ayan is part of a people who pride themselves on being 100 percent Muslim. To belong to Ayan's tribe is to be Muslim.

Ayan's personal identity, familial honor, relational standing, and social status are all inextricably intertwined with Islam. Simply put, if Ayan ever leaves her faith, she will immediately lose her life. If Ayan's family ever finds out that she is no longer a Muslim, they will slit her throat without question or hesitation… Ayan is not imaginary. She is a real woman I met who made a real choice to become a Christian— to die to herself and to live in Christ, no matter what it cost her. Because of her decision, she was forced to flee her family and became isolated from her friends. Yet she is now working strategically and sacrificially for the spread of the gospel among her people. The risk is high as every day she dies to herself all over again in order to live in Christ. Ayan's story is a clear reminder that the initial call to Christ is an inevitable call to die.[76]

The Call to Others-ness

The second part of this study recognizes that part of the model of the gospel call to the apostles was the call to "otherness"— a compassionate concern for the eternal destiny of others. As in Matthew 4:19, "Follow me, and I will make you fishers of men," the call by Christ, initially to the apostles, was a call towards otherness, a call to the concern for the eternal state of others. What a powerful illustration to speak to men whose vocation and livelihood was the fishing profession. Jesus was of course using something extremely familiar to them, in calling them to a new way of life, "catching men," "fishing for men" (of course, implied for men and women).

Let us unpack this idea again, the concept/the life direction of being a "fisher of men." Jesus used their vocation to show them He was calling them to a higher vocation, from a fishing they understood well to a Kingdom fishing, a higher fishing, if you will. The

---

[76]David Platt, *Follow Me: A Call to Die, A Call to Live*, (Carol Stream: Tyndale House, 2013), 1-2.

new direction of life the Lord Jesus now called them to was a catching of men and women for the eternal purposes of Almighty God. Certainly, they would have worked arduously as fishermen on the Sea of Galilee. They would have had to labor, perhaps competitively, at a task that was physically hard, smelly, dirty work; indeed, sometimes they had worked all night long and had caught nothing (Luke 5:5).

In Luke's account, the expression of Jesus, "Do not be afraid, from now on you will be catching men," the word *catching* is a "taking alive," it is "to catch or capture." The wording is a war term, to take captive (not to kill), it is used in 2 Timothy 2:25-26: "Correcting his opponents with gentleness. God may perhaps grant them repentance leading to a knowledge of the truth, and they may come to their senses and escape from the snare of the devil, after being captured by him to do his will." Such individuals have been taken captive by the devil.

This notion of fishing for men is a desire (by God's grace) to capture those who are currently enslaved in the kingdom of darkness. This is a catching of souls alive for the purposes of God. It is no wonder the fish became a favorite symbol for the early Christian community. It was the ixthus that was carved on many of the Christian tombs in the ancient catacombs down under the streets of Rome, in the initial days of the church.

The apostles were summoned by the Lord to live the new way of life. As fishers of men, one commentary described that this term "suggests care, patience, skill, besides habits of life fitted for the evidence of privation and fatigue."[77] So, this was no cushy clergy life, nor a sterile comfortable monastic environment separate from the world. It was a rigorous way of life seeking to win the lost, sick, and hurting to the cross-centered path.

Puritan pastor Thomas Boston in his book *The Art of Manfishing*, goes further into the notion of fighting for the souls of men and women. He writes (taking the analogy of the book further) the unregenerate are like fish in the water. His sub-points of the book include: "1) Sin is their home as water is the home of the fish"; 2) "Men are unprofitable as long as they remain in sin, just as fish are unprofitable as long as they remain in water." He expounds into sub-themes like: "There are many meshes to catch a fish (types of nets), so there are many invitations of the gospel to men."[78] He writes that it is Christ who makes fishers of men and that God compels the purpose in man to catch the poor souls of men and women with the gospel.

Many have thought—accomplished by the Holy Spirit—written books, and trained others in methods of how to be fishers of men, catchers of men. In the same way, as in the lives of those whom Jesus called in the apostles, as well as those He calls and compels to be manfishers today.

About the general commission of the manfishers, John Gill, an English Baptist pastor of an earlier time wrote, "the net they were to spread and cast was the gospel…The sea into which they were to cast the net was first Judea, and the whole world, the fish they were to catch were the souls of men."[79]

The believer today may be saying, "That's not my thing, I'm no evangelist." However, let me encourage you that though there are qualifications required for the pastor/elder of a church, there is no

---

[77]Joseph Exell and Henry D. M. Spence-Jones, *Commentary on Matthew, The Pulpit Commentary*. (Public Domain, 1897).

[78]Boston, *The Art of Man Fishing*.

[79]John Gill, *Exposition of the Entire Bible, Matthew* (Public Domain, 1816).

such requirement for those who would be "soul winners." You do not need a degree or certain type of ordination to do the work. Rather such gospel ministry requires the sincere compassion of what Paul was saying in 2 Corinthians 5:20: "Therefore, we are ambassadors for Christ, God making his appeal through us. We implore you on behalf of Christ, be reconciled to God."

....

It is as one man described this call of every believer,
"It is one beggar showing another beggar where to find bread."[80]

....

Another aspect found in Scripture and the church is that of God in a divine role in the fishing of souls. One of the earliest hymns in existence in the history of the Christian church was written by Clement of Alexandria (about AD 150-215). It sets forth an illustration of God as a divine fisherman, an imagery that is true to Scripture. It expresses:

Fisher of Men, the blessed, Out of the world's unrest
Out of sin's troubled sea, taking us, Lord with Thee
Out of the waves of strife, with bait of blissful life,
Drawing Thy nets to the shore, with choicest fish, good store.[81]

This imagery of God is found also in passages like the Kingdom parable of Matthew 13:47-50, where the kingdom of heaven is described as like a net that will be drawn in at the end of time. The angels will serve as agents of God, who will divide the profitable fish from the unprofitable fish.

---

[80]Often attributed to D.T. Niles, a Sri Lankan evangelist (1908-1970).

[81]Charles J. Ellicott, *A Bible Commentary for English Readers*, (Public Domain, 2019), From Matthew 4:19, quotation attributed to Clement of Alexandria.

Questions for Spiritual Formation:

1. Consider the passage from Matthew 16:24-25: "If anyone would come after me, let him deny himself and take up his cross and follow me. For whoever would save his life will lose it, but whoever loses his life for my sake will find it." Why are the words of Jesus in this text so difficult for westernized Christians to see are the fundamental call to follow Christ? (namely, self-denial and taking up our cross)

2. Why do believers in many highly persecuted areas of the world often consider staunch opposition, persecution, and suffering as normal in the Christian life, but Christians in the "free world" often see it as our right to not face adversity, persecution, and suffering?

3. How is the call by Christ to the original apostles and all believers today "I will make you fishers of men," a call towards othersness, a call to the concern for the eternal state of others?

4. Why can we consider the call to *fish for men*, just like one beggar showing another beggar where to find bread?

Softly and Tenderly
by Will L. Thompson

Softly and tenderly Jesus is calling,
calling for you and for me;
see, on the portals he's waiting and watching,
watching for you and for me.

Refrain:
Come home, come home;
you who are weary come home;
earnestly, tenderly, Jesus is calling,
calling, O sinner, come home!

Why should we tarry when Jesus is pleading,
pleading for you and for me?
Why should we linger and heed not his mercies,
mercies for you and for me?

Time is now fleeting, the moments are passing,
passing from you and from me;
shadows are gathering, deathbeds are coming,
coming for you and for me.

O for the wonderful love he has promised,
promised for you and for me!
Though we have sinned, he has mercy and pardon,
pardon for you and for me.[82]

---

[82] Will L.Thompson, *Softly and Tenderly*, (Public Domain, 1880).

Meditations for the Minefield of Life and Advancement of the Gospel

Chapter 9

Contending for the Historical Faith

One web site on "Defending a Medieval Castle" describes various defense features found in some of Britain's strongest castles. One can see the extensive measures taken to fortify a castle's defense.

> Medieval castles were built to be as defensive as possible. Every element of their architecture was designed to make sure that the castle was as strong as it could be, and could hold out against sieges – which could sometimes last months. Here are the different elements of castle defenses which rendered some fortresses truly impregnable...**The Outer Curtain Wall** -The 'curtain wall' was the vast stone wall which wrapped around the outside of a castle.
>
> As you might imagine, it's called a 'curtain' because it covered everything within. This wall was the main layer of defense, and it tended to be incredibly strong – for example, the curtain wall of Caerphilly Castle in Wales was more than 2 meters (that's more than 6ft) thick. Usually, the center of the wall was made of rough rocks and rubble, and the outer parts were made of gigantic stones, laid like modern-day bricks. This method of construction gave the 'core' of the wall extra strength, and it helped it to withstand battering-rams and missiles.
>
> **Moats and Water Defenses**-Many castles were surrounded by manmade ditches which were then filled with water, and

turned into moats. Incidentally, the water in the moat would have been truly disgusting — it was stagnant and all the waste from the castle toilets was tipped straight in. However, in Medieval times, everything would have smelled terrible — so the vile moat wouldn't in itself have put off attackers! The moat served a number of useful purposes. Firstly, it meant that attackers couldn't get too close to the outer castle walls. This prevented them from being able to use battering-rams and made it harder to be accurate when flinging missiles.

It also made it easier for archers in the castle to aim at on-comers. Imagine you were an archer standing on high: if there was someone at the foot of the castle directly below, it would have been too difficult to fire at them accurately. A moat meant that attackers couldn't get too close — so it was easier to pick them off with arrows. The moat had other advantages, too. It made it tricky for anyone to burrow beneath the castle, or undermine the outer walls."[83]

As the strategic defense of castles was at one time a way of life for families, towns, and cities that indwelt the castle walls, so the text considered in this chapter concerns the defense of the divinely bestowed gospel truth. This is the truth that was passed along by the ancients as the *once for all delivered to the saints faith*. This was from the outset, the heaven-sent truth that was waited for, and was to be cherished, defended, taught to every subsequent generation, and proclaimed to the nations.

---

[83]Exploring Castles, Medieval Castle Defence: Defending a Castle, Castle Designs, http://www.exploring-castles.com/castle_designs/medieval_castle_defence/.

"Beloved, although I was very eager to write to you about our common salvation, I found it necessary to write appealing to you to contend for the faith that was once for all delivered to the saints." (Jude 1:3)

This brief epistle is considered by many to have been written by the half-brother of Jesus Christ, due to the information given in the introduction: "Jude, a servant of Jesus Christ and brother of James, to those who are called, beloved in God the Father and kept for Jesus Christ" (Jude 1). It has been established that he must be the brother of the man James, the leader of the church in Jerusalem and the half-brother of the Lord Jesus. This is the strongest view and many Bible teachers agree on this.

Here Jude seems to be writing his epistle to a small group of churches known to him. These churches would have circulated his writings around and shared the readership, as he did not designate any one particular church as the recipient of the letter. As verse 3 is read, it is noticeable that he indeed sees the necessity to write to them this letter of warning, which is a response to the situation of wicked men who had crept into the churches, causing damage to the spiritual well-being of the congregations. He writes, "For certain people have crept in unnoticed who long ago were designated for this condemnation, ungodly people, who pervert the grace of our God into sensuality and deny our only Master and Lord, Jesus Christ" (Jude 1:4).

He further comments about the wicked men who have snuck in, reflecting on the judgment of God upon the homosexual wickedness of the past, "just as Sodom and Gomorrah and the surrounding cities, which likewise indulged in sexual immorality and pursued unnatural desire, serve as an example by undergoing a punishment of eternal fire" (verse 7). As well as in verse 11: "Woe to them! For they walked in the way of Cain and abandoned themselves for the sake of gain to Balaam's error and perished in Korah's rebellion." And again in verse 16: "These are grumblers, malcontents, following their own sinful desires; they are loud-mouthed boasters, showing favoritism to gain advantage." Jude uses highly descriptive language here to

118

describe these individuals who had wickedly infiltrated the beloved church of the living God.

The Purpose of the Need to Declare

So, verse 3 shows Jude is writing to a specific group of believers or group of churches whom he begins to address by calling the "beloved." He uses a very affectionate term here, addressing the believers whom he is writing to warn. He uses the Greek word *agape* (αγαπητοι). This is the self-sacrificial love spoken of in the New Testament; it is the love that describes God the Father's love for God the Son (John 3:35). The apostle Paul uses the description of this kind of love in 1 Corinthians 13, the treasured passage on biblical love. Paul writes:

> Love is patient and kind; love does not envy or boast; it is not arrogant or rude. It does not insist on its own way; it is not irritable or resentful; it does not rejoice at wrongdoing, but rejoices with the truth. Love bears all things, believes all things, hopes all things, endures all things. Love never ends. As for prophecies, they will pass away; as for tongues, they will cease; as for knowledge, it will pass away. (1 Cor. 13:4-8).

Jude is saying to the New Testament community of Christ that he was serving, "I love you with a self-sacrificial love that never ends, and therefore I am writing you this letter of warning." He is declaring to them that with "all haste" he is writing to them. He is expressing the important urgency of the situation here, essentially he is writing to them that they may hear about the urgent issue at hand, as fast as he can get it to them. Furthermore, he states that it is concerning theirs and his common salvation. He is telling them that the matter of discussion, which is so urgent, is that matter of their common salvation. The NIV states that it is about "the salvation we share." This is their mutual salvation, the very same salvation that believers know and share today.

The term "common" is used in Acts: "And all who believed were together and had all things in common. And they were selling their possessions and belongings and distributing the proceeds to all, as any had need" (2:44-45). In the New Testament community, the believers shared a common life because of their common salvation. Acts speaks of the precious salvation which they shared in common, that which had bound them together in unity. It is the very same salvation that believers share today wherever true, genuine, Christian fellowship occurs and wherever genuine disciples and followers of Jesus Christ gather. To share in this common salvation is to enter into such fellowship as in John 3:5, to be born again and to be brought into the Kingdom of God.

The Urgent Need to Appeal

Turning to the second portion of Jude 3, Jude begins to shift to the urgent need that he was compelled to address. It was about the salvation that believers share, that Jude says, "I found it necessary to write appealing to you," or as the KJV reads, "It was needful for me to write unto you." The necessity or compulsion is the matter that Jude is giving as to why he had to write to them. Further, to grasp this *necessity* to which he was speaking of, another usage of this *necessity* is found in 1 Corinthians 9:16 where the apostle Paul says in the KJV, "For *necessity* is laid upon me; yea woe is unto me, if I preach not the gospel" (emphasis added). Or as the NASB translates the word *compulsion* in the text, "For I am under *compulsion*; for woe is me if I do not preach the gospel" (emphasis added). Jude absolutely had to write the letter. Again, Jude 1:3 pleads, "Beloved, although I was very eager to write to you about our common salvation, I found it necessary to write appealing to you to contend for the faith that was once for all delivered to the saints."

It is as if he dropped all that he was doing to get his letter to them, like a shepherd chasing a wolf that was immediately spotted entering into the sheepfold incurring danger upon the flock. One commentator writes, "Jude was busy on another subject when he received the news of a fresh danger to the Church, which he felt it his duty to meet at once. Whether he lived to carry out his earlier design, and whether it was of the nature of a treatise or of an epistle, we know not."[84] Jude was deeply convicted that time was of the essence in this matter; this is the compulsion of a concerned pastor.

As the verse unfolds, the remainder of the verse is an appeal to the recipients of the letter for what Jude deeply wants them to do. The appeal is making towards the believers is admonishing, exhorting, or urging them to pursue some course of conduct. His appeal is that they would do something specific due to the situation of the wicked men infiltrating the church. Furthermore, that something specific is that they would "contend earnestly for the faith that was once for all delivered to the saints."

The wording translated *appeal* or *exhort* here is literally that Jude was compelled by this urgent need to be "the one who is exhorting them." Other synonyms used for this word are less familiar but still descriptive like *imploring* and *beseeching*. This is a calling them to the urgent responsibility of protecting the gospel of Christ. In colonial times the early Americans had minute men ready at a moments notice to ride by horseback calling the people to arms because they were being attacked. This is the idea of *beseeching* someone, just as Paul Revere and his co-patriots rode through Lexington, Massachusettes crying out, 'The Redcoats are coming, the Redcoats are coming.' They were under attack, and he *implored* or *exhorted* the citizens to defend their homes and loved ones.

---

[84]W. Robertson Nicoll, *The Expositors Greek Testament*, (Public Domain, 1896).

121

The Once for All Delivered to the Saints Faith

Turning to the content of the "faith that was once for all delivered to the saints," this is the faith that Jude exhorted to his readers of the past, and down through the ages to contend earnestly for. Scripture attests to what the faith was that had been delivered to the apostles and early believers. This faith, which was once for all delivered to the saint is a faith described concisely in 1 Corinthians 15:3-7:

For I delivered to you as of first importance what I also received: that Christ died for our sins in accordance with the Scriptures, that he was buried, that he was raised on the third day in accordance with the Scriptures, and that he appeared to Cephas, then to the twelve. Then he appeared to more than five hundred brothers at one time, most of whom are still alive, though some have fallen asleep. Then he appeared to James, then to all the apostles. Last of all, as to one untimely born, he appeared also to me.

In this text, the apostle Paul uses the very same word for "delivered," in essence he had delivered to the saints in Corinth the faith that was first delivered to him and the other apostles. As well, the apostle Paul refers to this concept of the initial "standard" of gospel teaching that he had received in Romans 6:17, "But thanks be to God, that you who were once slaves of sin have become obedient from the heart to the standard of teaching to which you were committed." Paul speaks similarly throughout his New Testament writings, such as Ephesians 4:5, that there is "one Lord, one faith, one baptism." And again as he exhorted the Galatian Church, "As we have said before, so now I say again: If anyone is preaching to you a gospel contrary to the one you received, let him be accursed." (Gal. 1:9)

In other words, the precious "once for all delivered to the saints" (Jude 1:3) faith is the historical gospel message of Christ crucified that Paul had received. This timeless truth of the gospel is what Bible Commentator, D. Edmund Hiebert writes, "The faith for which believers are to earnestly to contend is the message of the gospel, that body of Christian truth that brings salvation to the soul that receives it."[85]

The historicity of our faith in invaluable, and the church must heed this rich history we share. John Piper writes on Jude 3:

> The faith that we cherish was preserved for us with the blood of hundreds of reformers. From 1555 to 1558 Queen Mary, the Catholic ruler in England, had 288 Protestant reformers burned at the stake—men like John Rogers, John Hooper, Rowland Taylor, Robert Ferrar, John Bradford, Nicholas Ridley, Hugh Latimer, and Thomas Cranmer. And why were they burned? Because they stood by a truth—the truth that the real presence of Jesus' body is not in the Eucharist but in heaven at the Father's right hand. For that truth they endured the excruciating pain of being burned alive. The blood of the martyrs is a powerful testimony that the faith once for all delivered to the saints is worth contending for. But there is evidence of this right here in verse 3. Jude says that what he is really writing about is *our common salvation*.[86]

The Duty of the Gospel Worker

What are the believers to do that Jude is writing to, and what are believers to do today? Looking at the central idea of the verse, and

---

[85]D. Edmund Hiebert, Second Peter and Jude: An Expositional Commentary, (Greenville: Unusual Productions, 1989), 216-221.

[86]John Piper, "Contend for the Faith," *Desiring God Ministries*, http://www.desiringgod.org/messages/contend-for-the-faith.

for which Jude felt burdened to write, he pleads, "Contend earnestly." The Greek verb that this English phrase comes from is one word, επαγωνιζεσθαι, which has as a root, "to agonize," meaning "to strive." Robert Mounce states about the term, it means "to contend strenuously in defense of" something. [87]

Hiebert writes that this word: "was much used in connection with athletic contests to describe a strenuous struggle to overcome an opponent, as in a wrestling match."[88] Additionally, it means generally to strive in a conflict, contest, debate, or lawsuit. This contending earnestly or vigorously defending the once for all delivered to the saints is called for by other authors of Scripture as well.

Other examples of the notion of defending the message of the Christ crucified and the wider corpus of Scripture comes from the apostle Peter: "But in your hearts honor Christ the Lord as holy, always being prepared to make a defense to anyone who asks you for a reason for the hope that is in you; yet do it with gentleness and respect" (1 Peter 3:15). This also admonishes the people of God to heed the responsibility to take a stand for the faith. We are to defend the faith, though with gentleness and respect for others. The word *defense* in the verse above comes from the original Greek term απολογιαν, from where the English word *apologetics* is derived, referring to the study of defending the gospel by reasoning with others from Scripture.

As well, Paul seems to favor the concept of defending the faith. There are two examples from 1 Timothy. One is 1 Timothy 6:12: "Fight the good fight of the faith. Take hold of the eternal life to which you were called and about which you made the good confession in the presence of many witnesses." This verse has the same root word for *contend earnestly* as in Jude 1:3, again the English

---

[87]Robert Mounce, Mounce Concise Greek-English Dictionary of the New Testament. "Επαγωνιζεσθαι."

[88]Hiebert, *Jude*, 218.

word *agonize* is derived from this. Literally, Paul is exhorting Timothy to *agonize the good agony* of the faith, he was challenging him to engage in a fierce struggle like that of overcoming an opponent.

The second example is from 1 Timothy 6:20-21 where Paul admonishes Timothy: "O Timothy, guard the deposit entrusted to you. Avoid the irreverent babble and contradictions of what is falsely called 'knowledge,' for by professing it some have swerved from the faith." Paul is reminding Timothy of the invaluable treasure of the gospel. It is as if he is pleading to him, "Timothy, guard it with your life, do not allow those who have wandered away from Christ distort, pervert, or change it in any way.

Another illustration of this same root word comes again from Paul in 1 Thessalonians 2:1-2 where the ESV translates *conflict*. It was the conflict Paul experienced while bringing the gospel to them:

> For you yourselves know, brothers, that our coming to you was not in vain. But though we had already suffered and been shamefully treated at Philippi, as you know, we had boldness in our God to declare to you the gospel of God in the midst of much conflict.

Notice Paul is saying they suffered and were treated shamefully, and in the middle of much *conflict* they were bold to preach the gospel. We must consider that often a struggle, persecution, or conflict that we will need to push through is part of the Christian life, and much a part of the misesteeming to others.

Regarding the actual *contending* or struggling for the Christian faith, consider again the comments Piper has on this responsibility of *contending* for our faith. He states:

> When it comes to the actual *contending* Jude says in verses 22–23, "And convince some, who doubt; save some, by snatching them out of the fire; on some have mercy with fear, hating even the garment spotted by the flesh." At least two things are evident here. One is that *contending*

125

sometimes involves an intellectual effort to change the way a person thinks: "Convince some, who doubt." The other is that *contending* sometimes involves moral reclamation: go after them into the mess where their perverse ideas have taken them, and snatch them back to safety even while you hate what they are doing. In reality these things always go together: an effort to change the mind and an effort to change the morals. *Contending* for the faith is never merely an academic exercise. It is never merely mental. Because the source of all false doctrine is the pride of the man's hearts not the weakness of his mind.[89]

This is the responsibility of the believer, yet it must be cultivated and pursued, and with it comes the need to understand how others see life, the need to understand their world view and to to listen and to engage them in understanding that a bridge for the gospel may be built with communication to their mind and heart.

---

[89]Piper, *Contend.*

Questions for Spiritual Formation:

1. How is the necessity that Jude felt like a shepherd chasing a wolf that was immediately spotted entering into the sheepfold incurring danger upon the flock?

2. How would you describe the fundamental content of the "faith that was once for all delivered to the saints"?

3. Why would it be that there are actual Christians and entire churches today that do not sense the conviction towards this gospel duty to *contend earnestly* for the faith?

4. The chapter closes with a quote from the Bible teacher, John Piper, in reference to Jude 1:22-23: "Have mercy on those who doubt; save others by snatching them out of the fire; to others show mercy with fear, hating even the garment stained by the flesh." Piper says:

5. At least two things are evident here. One is that *contending* sometimes involves an intellectual effort to change the way a person thinks: 'Convince some, who doubt.' The other is that *contending* sometimes involves moral reclamation: go after them into the mess where their perverse ideas have taken them, and snatch them back to safety even while you hate what they are doing."

6. What are examples of some who may be *doubting* versus those who desperately need to be *snatched out of the fire?*

I Know Whom I Have Believed
by Daniel W. Whittle

I know not why God's wondrous grace
To me He hath made known,
Nor why, unworthy, Christ in love
Redeemed me for His own.

Refrain:
But "I know Whom I have believed,
And am persuaded that He is able
To keep that which I've committed
Unto Him against that day."

I know not how this saving faith
To me He did impart,
Nor how believing in His Word
Wrought peace within my heart.

I know not how the Spirit moves,
Convincing men of sin,
Revealing Jesus through the Word,
Creating faith in Him.

I know not what of good or ill
May be reserved for me,
Of weary ways or golden days,
Before His face I see.

I know not when my Lord may come,
At night or noonday fair,
Nor if I walk the vale with Him,
Or meet Him Him in the air.[90]

---

[90]Daniel W. Whittle, *I Know Whom I Have Believed*, (Public Domain, 1883).

Chapter 10

Combating Worldly Appetites

Two brothers lived in the Harlem area of New York in the early 1900's, Homer and Langley Collyer, in a way their lives tell a very powerful illustration of the extremes that human beings can go to in their greed, materialism and fearful obsession about worldly possessions. Both of the Collyer brothers were very intelligent and graduated from Columbia. Homer finished in 1904, he earned an MA, LLB and LLM. Langley had degrees in both chemistry and mechanical engineering. Homer practiced Law, but Langley dedicating his life to music did not have employment. The story of their lives is an account of extreme hoarding.

It was there, barricaded in a sanctuary of junk, that the blind and bedridden Homer Collyer lived with his devoted younger brother, Langley, the elderly scions of an upper-class Manhattan family. And it was there that they amassed one of the world's legendary collections of urban junk, a collection so extraordinary that their accomplishment, such as it was, came to represent the ultimate New York cautionary tale. The Collyer brothers' saga confirms a New Yorker's worst nightmare: crumpled people living in crumpled rooms with their crumpled possessions, the crowded chaos of the city refracted in their homes. It's not that Gothamites hoard more than other people; it's that they have less room to hoard in. Even now, after more than a half century, the Collyer name still reso-nates.[91]

The New York County public administrator assumed leader-ship in the deconstruction of the hoard. Movers were hired that began with anything of value beginning with a law library of 2500 law books (a mere fraction of the books contained in the house). As we, they found "family oil portraits...they found Mrs. Collyer's hope chests, jammed with unused piece goods, silks, wool, damask and brocade; three bolts of embroidered white curtain material, each con-taining 54 yards, that had never been unwrapped; and a batch of fine linen dish towels, stamped "Collyer," that had never been used." As well, were found:

> telephone directories, three revolvers, two rifles, a shotgun, ammunition, a bayonet and a saber, a half-dozen toy trains, toy tops, a toy airplane, 14 upright and grand pianos, cornets, bugles, an accordion, a trombone, a banjo; tin cans, chande-liers, tapestries, a portrait camera, enlarger, lenses and tri-pods, a bowling ball in a canvas bag, bicycles and bicycle lamps, a rolled-up 100-foot rug runner, a 9-foot-tall mahog-any clock with a music box inside and pastel painted figures on the broad face; 13 ornate mantel clocks...13 Oriental rugs, heavily ornate Victorian oil lamps and vases, white plaster portrait busts and picture frames...five violins, at least two dating from the 18th century, two organs and scores of 7-inch gramophone records dating from 1898... They found sheets in braille from Homer's failed attempts to learn the system. And they found a certificate of merit for punctuality and good conduct awarded to Langley at Public School 69, 125 W.

[91]Franx Lidz, "The Paper Chase," *The New York Times*. https://ar-chive.vn/20120713235104/http://query.nytimes.com/gst/full-page.html?res=9C07E2D91231F935A15753C1A9659C8B63#selection-331.0-335.75.

54th St., for the week ending April 19, 1895. These things merely salted the vast sea of junk and paper.[92]

The dismantleing of the hoard eventually uncovered the corpse of the elder of the two brothers, Homer. Records show there was a remaining search for the younger of the brothers, Langley:

> The hunt for Langley began, and authorities searched for him as far away as Atlantic City. A disturbing realization took place three weeks later, unfortunately, when Langley's body was found ten feet from his older brother's. Because of the vast amount of garbage in the house, his body wasn't unearthed until then. Langley had been crushed to death by one of his many booby-traps that he had made to deter people's entry into their palace of junk. Langley actually had died first. He was crushed while bringing food to his elder brother, who was blind. Langley fed Homer a diet of one hundred oranges per week to try and restore his sight. Believing that the diet of oranges would restore Homer's vision, Langley also saved every newspaper so that Homer could eventually read them when his sight returned.[93]

More than 100 tons of trash was removed from the Collyer brothers' house. This included items like human pickled organs, the chassis of an old Model T, fourteen pianos (both grand and upright), hundreds of yards of unused silks and fabric, the folding top of a horse-drawn carriage, and more than 25,000 books.[94] Robert F. Wagner Jr., the city's commissioner of Housing and Buildings   led the

---

[92]William Bryk, "The Collyer Brothers," *The New York Sun*, (Apr 13, 2005.

[93]Kerry McQueeney, "The ultimate hoarders: Extraordinary story of the two reclusive brothers found dead side by side under tons of junk in New York mansion in 1947," *Daily Mail.com*,
https://www.dailymail.co.uk/ushome/index.html.

condemnationand demplition of the build (era 1947-1948).[95] One New York Times article summarized account of the materialistic obsession of the Collyer brothers as, "a depressing tale of two shut-ins who withdrew from life to preside over their own 'kingdom of rubble.'"[96]

The tragedy of the story above all else may be found in that the brothers were so paranoid people would steal their earthly treasures, that they made traps to ensnare any potential thieves. Though the story of one brother compassionately devoting himself to the care of the other is inspiring, sadly it was surrounded by their fear of anything jeopardizing all the worldly goods that they had fervently hoarded.

Do not love the world or the things in the world. If anyone loves the world, the love of the Father is not in him. For all that is in the world—the desires of the flesh and the desires of the eyes and pride of life—is not from the Father but is from the world. And the world is passing away along with its desires, but whoever does the will of God abides forever (1 John 2:15-17).

The aged apostle John, it is understood, wrote the letter of 1 John near the end of his life, and that he was not put to death for his faith (as the other apostles are recorded to have been). The loving apostle wrote much about loving others, loving God, and God loving us. It has been written down in history that he was tortured for Jesus by being boiled alive in oil. History says he was delivered from death by a miracle, spared from the boiling oil. He wrote the Gospel of

---

[95]Bryk, "The Collyer Brothers."
[96]Michiko Kakutani, "How Did they end up that way?," *New York Times: Books* (Aug 31, 2009). https://archive.nytimes.com/www.nytimes.com/2009/09/01/books/01kakutani.html.

John, 1ˢᵗ, 2ⁿᵈ, and 3ʳᵈ John, and the book of the Revelation of Jesus.[97, 98]

In this chapter, we will look at teaching from the apostle John on how Christians are called by God to not love the ways of this world. First John 2:15-17 then can be looked at in 3 parts:

1) do not love the world;
2) the ways of the world are not from God; and
3) the ways of God are forever.

Do Not Love the World

Looking then at the first point, drawn like water from a well from 1 John 2:15, which reads, "Do not love the world or the things in the world. If anyone loves the world, the love of the Father is not in him." So, to not love the world then is the objective that John is calling all believers to. In 1 John, overall, John provides fatherly guidance on what it means to be a true Christian. It could be said then that a genuine Christian is someone who does not love this passing world. The question that would naturally be considered from this is, "What does it mean to love the world?" and the implication is we should NOT love the world? It must be made clear then that when John writes the word *world*, and when he speaks of things of the world that must not be loved by the Christian, he speaks of a certain type of love or affection for the morally evil ways of this world.

---

[97]Michael Patton, "What Happened to the Twelve Apostles? How do Their Deaths Prove Easter?," *Credo House*, https://credohouse.org/blog/what-happened-to-the-twelve-apostles-how-do-their-deaths-prove-easter#james, other historical documents, individuals are involved in this process. (Ex. "As Hippolytus tells us, Andrew was hanged on an olive tree at Patrae, a town in Achaia.").

[98]John Foxe, *Fox's Book of Martyrs*, https://www.whitehorseme-dia.com/docs/FOXS_BOOK_OF_MARTYRS.pdf, 1-4.

This love is the supreme type of love by which we must love God. The world should never receive this same type of love, by which we should be loving and adoring almighty God. Again, the world that John is speaking of here is one of moral evil. The ways of this non-loving-God world, do not seek His wisdom, and move against His ways. There is a system of evil in this world led by Satan, and opposed to the Kingdom of Jesus Christ. The system of this world is trying to seduce you and your children to love and lust after its ways; and it is trying to coerce believers to turn away from following Jesus.

Jesus states things in a bolder manner, teaching that the world absolutely hated Him, and may likewise hate all of us who follow Him today. Remember Jesus said that He has chosen believers from out of the world, but this world hated him and crucified him. Likewise the world will usually hate the Christ- follower as well, the same way it hated Jesus. (John 15:18-20)

Notice again, the Lord Jesus is saying that the world hated Him, and really if the world hated Him if we go out into the world with the message He has given, the world may very well respond to us with hate. The remaining part of the verse goes on to read that if anyone loves the world, the love of the Father is not in them. As alluded to earlier, the issue at hand is that believers cannot say they love God and then have a love affair with the world at the same time. These two concepts are contradictory— "loving the world" and "loving God."

This loving the world is a loving of the things of the world in the same way that you love and worship God. The way that one loves the things or ways of the world more than they love God is described in 1 John 2:16: "For all that is in the world—the desires of the flesh and the desires of the eyes and pride of life—is not from the Father but is from the world." This is a description of the things of the world that are not from God.

An example of a man who loved the world and the things of the world and didn't love God is Nebuchadnezzar of Babylon. From Daniel is found:

All this came upon King Nebuchadnezzar. At the end of twelve months he was walking on the roof of the royal palace of Babylon, and the king answered and said, "Is not this great Babylon, which I have built by my mighty power as a royal residence and for the glory of my majesty?"

While the words were still in the king's mouth, there fell a voice from heaven, "O King Nebuchadnezzar, to you it is spoken: The kingdom has departed from you, and you shall be driven from among men, and your dwelling shall be with the beasts of the field. And you shall be made to eat grass like an ox, and seven periods of time shall pass over you, until you know that the Most High rules the kingdom of men and gives it to whom he will." Immediately the word was fulfilled against Nebuchadnezzar. He was driven from among men and ate grass like an ox, and his body was wet with the dew of heaven till his hair grew as long as eagles' feathers, and his nails were like birds' claws. At the end of the days I, Nebuchadnezzar, lifted my eyes to heaven, and my reason returned to me, and I blessed the Most High, and praised and honored him who lives forever, for his dominion is an everlasting dominion, and his kingdom endures from generation to generation; all the inhabitants of the earth are accounted as nothing, and he does according to his will among the host of heaven and among the inhabitants of the earth; and none can stay his hand or say to him, "What have you done?"

At the same time my reason returned to me, and for the glory of my kingdom, my majesty and splendor returned to me. My counselors and my lords sought me, and I was established in my kingdom, and still more greatness was added to me. Now I, Nebuchadnezzar, praise and extol and honor the King of heaven, for all his works are right and his ways are just; and those who walk in pride he is able to humble. (Daniel 4:28-37)

King Nebuchadnezzar was carried away by an evil lust for the ways of the world, he loved himself so much, and desired his own glory, and praised himself and not God for the kingdom that he had built for himself. God brought him down to the dust, teaching him a complete and thorough attitude of humility. As the passage states, he was made like an animal, lived and ate like an animal, and became a madman for 7 years until he bowed and gave thanks to the Creator God, and gave proper honor to the Lord for all the things that he enjoyed and was responsible for in life.

The Ways of the World Are not from God

Look again at verse 16 of 1 John 2: "For all that is in the world—the desires of the flesh and the desires of the eyes and pride of life—is not from the Father but is from the world." This second point—the ways of the world are not from God—has already been alluded to and reminds us that the Bible says the ways of the world are to live to satisfy the lusts of the flesh, and eyes, and to feed our own human pride (a sinful and self-absorbed pride). There are things that are appropriate to desire and to pray for, but when motivations are corrupt, longings depraved, and lust unbridled with no self-control, the items which we covet after have become idols of our heart and our desire has become absolutely sinful.

Something good or wholesome in life, when inordinately desired and coveted—such as a marriage partner for example, or even a new vehicle or bicycle—becomes sinful. The object of your affections may grow to be an evil desire if it is not scrutinized by the Word of God and not submitted to God, with the prayer: *If it be the will of God, let it be done.* (James 4:13-17) Similarly, though considered worse, the compulsive desires of the gambler, alcohol or drug addict, the sexual addict, or even those obsessed with power, promotion, or money can become enslaved to a destructive form of idolatry.

Regarding the "pride of life," it is a significant theme in Scripture, meaning essentially a braggadocio, or a boastful pride. It is literally, "originally, *empty, braggart talk* or *display*; *swagger*; and thence an insolent and vain assurance in one's own resources, or in the stability of earthly things, which issues in a contempt of divine laws."[99] Self-reflectively, this pride is lying to oneself and others, and exaggerating about oneself to impress people. Again, considering King Nebuchadnezzar, God had blessed his kingdom, lavish in common grace that all enjoyed, and that the Jews specifically benefitted from. Yet the wicked king deceived himself, believing he had accomplished it all by his own savvy and personal greatness. He saw it all had been completed from his own humanistic intelligence; he congratulated and thanked himself: "And the king answered and said, 'Is not this great Babylon, which I have built by my mighty power as a royal residence and for the glory of my majesty?'"

Thus God saw it necessary for His glory and sovereign purposes to humble him and remove from him all his arrogance. Repeatedly, pride is found in Scripture as that element which contradicts the humility necessary to walk in a right relationship with the Lord. It is a qualification for a church elder: "He must not be a recent convert, or he may become puffed up with conceit and fall into the condemnation of the devil" (1 Tim. 3:6). Other leaders fell in history to the arrogance of sinful pride. The prophet Ezekiel was called to prophesy against the king of Tyre who exemplified the very embodiment of Satan and exists in Scripture for all time as a model of the supremacy of hellish haughtiness:

> Moreover, the word of the LORD came to me: 'Son of man, raise a lamentation over the king of Tyre, and say to him, thus says the Lord GOD: You were the signet of perfection, full of wisdom and perfect in beauty. You were in Eden, the garden of God; every precious stone was your covering, sardius, topaz, and diamond, beryl, onyx, and jasper, sapphire,

---

[99]Marvin R. Vincent, *Vincent's Word Studies*. "pride of life."

emerald, and carbuncle; and crafted in gold were your settings and your engravings. On the day that you were created they were prepared. You were an anointed guardian cherub. I placed you; you were on the holy mountain of God; in the midst of the stones of fire you walked. You were blameless in your ways from the day you were created, till unrighteousness was found in you. In the abundance of your trade you were filled with violence in your midst, and you sinned; so I cast you as a profane thing from the mountain of God, and I destroyed you, O guardian cherub, from the midst of the stones of fire. Your heart was proud because of your beauty; you corrupted your wisdom for the sake of your splendor. I cast you to the ground; I exposed you before kings, to feast their eyes on you. By the multitude of your iniquities, in the unrighteousness of your trade you profaned your sanctuaries; so I brought fire out from your midst; it consumed you, and I turned you to ashes on the earth in the sight of all who saw you. All who know you among the peoples are appalled at you; you have come to a dreadful end and shall be no more forever' (Ezek. 28:11-19).

It is imperative to not be caught in woeful ignorance about the wiles of satanic pride. If you are reading this book today, please take heed and pray that God will purge the dross of sinful pride from your life (Prov. 6:16-19).

The Ways of God Are Forever

In considering the last thought of this study from 1 John 2:15-17 on the eternality of the ways of God, verse 17 in review explains: "And the world is passing away along with its desires, but whoever does the will of God abides forever." Here are two things focused upon: 1) something that is passing away; and 2) something that will last forever. Therefore, the ways of the world, including the lusts of worldly living, are passing away, but the ways of Almighty God, the will of God, and the Word of God will last forever. The ways of evil of the world, and the ways of covetous lust with our eyes and flesh chasing after things we greedily desire in life—this is passing away. It is a change that is taking place and will ultimately take place as the program of God advances.

Looking at the words of Jesus, it is communicated that there is absolutely something that will never pass away. It is the Word of our God that will never pass away (not even the smallest hint of it.) (Matt. 5:18). So, Jesus talked about heaven and earth that will one day pass away; it is this present world that is temporary. Second Peter 3:10 also addresses this: "But the day of the Lord will come like a thief, and then the heavens will pass away with a roar, and the heavenly bodies will be burned up and dissolved, and the earth and the works that are done on it will be exposed."

Therefore, the earth will one day be totally consumed, dissolved by a fervent heat of fire, and we are called to be a people "waiting for and hastening the coming of the day of God, because of which the heavens will be set on fire and dissolved, and the heavenly bodies will melt as they burn! But according to his promise we are waiting for new heavens and a new earth in which righteousness dwells" (2 Peter 3:12-13). God is going to burn up the world one day, it is indeed temporary. The saints consequently are to look for new heavens and a new earth where righteousness dwells, without sin, pain, sorrow, or death.

The bottom line is that only God's Will, God's Ways, and God's Word are going to last forever. There are many verses throughout Scripture that testify about what God says will happen. The ways of God will stand forever; the will of God for this world will not be stopped or changed. This is our Father's world, and His people are protected by His promises. One representative verse that comforts us along these lines is Isaiah 46:9-10:

> Remember the former things of old; for I am God, and there is no other; I am God, and there is none like me, declaring the end from the beginning and from ancient times things not

139

yet done, saying, 'My counsel shall stand, and I will accomplish all my purpose.'

Another account from Scripture that summarizes much of the sentiments of this chapter comes from the life of King Solomon in his auto-biographical book of Ecclesiastes:

> I said in my heart, "Come now, I will test you with pleasure; enjoy yourself." But behold, this also was vanity. I said of laughter, "It is mad," and of pleasure, "What use is it?" I searched with my heart how to cheer my body with wine—my heart still guiding me with wisdom—and how to lay hold on folly, till I might see what was good for the children of man to do under heaven during the few days of their life. I made great works. I built houses and planted vineyards for myself. I made myself gardens and parks, and planted in them all kinds of fruit trees. I made myself pools from which to water the forest of growing trees. I bought male and female slaves, and had slaves who were born in my house. I had also great possessions of herds and flocks, more than any who had been before me in Jerusalem. I also gathered for myself silver and gold and the treasure of kings and provinces. I got singers, both men and women, and many concubines, the delight of the sons of man. So I became great and surpassed all who were before me in Jerusalem. Also my wisdom remained with me. And whatever my eyes desired I did not keep from them. I kept my heart from no pleasure, for my heart found pleasure in all my toil, and this was my reward for all my toil. Then I considered all that my hands had done and the toil I had expended in doing it, and behold, all was vanity and a striving after wind, and there was nothing to be gained under the sun (Eccl. 2:1-11).

Here the king had completely given over the demands of his sinful self-indulgence, all for his own pleasure, acquiring all for his pleasure, to consume it upon his pleasure. By his own testimony, "And whatever my eyes desired I did not keep from them. I kept my heart from no pleasure" (verse 10), he zealously pursued the lust of the flesh and lust of the eyes, and pride of life. As he sinfully indulged himself, God mercifully allowed him to discover that apart from God all was existentially void. He wrote, "Then I considered all that my hands had done and the toil I had expended in doing it, and behold, all was vanity and a striving after wind, and there was nothing to be gained under the sun" (verse 11). He ultimately felt experientially empty and that he had been "striving after wind." This is a weighty and illustrative expression of futility. Nothing satisfies the soul of man apart from the saving relationship with God through faith in Jesus Christ. Solomon came to the emptiness of this world's pursuits and ultimately wrote: "The end of the matter; all has been heard. Fear God and keep his commandments, for this is the whole duty of man" (Eccl. 12:13).

Questions for Spiritual Formation:

1. How would the story included about the hoarding lifestyle of Homer and Langley Collyer be considered relevant to worldly appetites?

2. What does it mean to love the world?

3. Why is the sinful pride described in 1 Tim. 3:6), which means *blinded with arrogance, braggadocio* or *self-conceit,* many times seen as being virtuous? How can we discern between this arrogant pride and being involved in our world/society in a humble way, so that we pursue the qualification of true spiritual leadership? As Scripture teaches, "He must not be a recent convert, or he may become puffed up with conceit and fall into the condemnation of the devil" (1 Tim. 3:6).

Give Me Jesus
by Fanny Crosby

Take the world, but give me Jesus,
All its joys are but a name;

But His love abideth ever,
Through eternal years the same.

Take the world, but give me Jesus,
Sweetest comfort of my soul;
With my Savior watching o'er me,
I can sing though billows roll.

Take the world, but give me Jesus,
Let me view His constant smile;
Then throughout my pilgrim journey
Light will cheer me all the while.

Take the world, but give me Jesus;
In His cross my trust shall be,
Till, with clearer, brighter vision,
Face to face my Lord I see.

Refrain:

Oh, the height and depth of mercy!
Oh, the length and breadth of love!
Oh, the fullness of redemption,
Pledge of endless life above![100]

---

[100]Fanny Crosby, *Give Me Jesus*, (Public Domain, 1879).

Chapter 11

The Good Fight of the Believer

Boxing has a long, storied history. Its origins can be traced as far back as ancient Mesopotamia, where a terracotta relief was discovered that depicts men boxing. Surely, though, boxing is much older, given the fact that the act of striking another with one's fist is simply a basic defensive (as well as offensive) mechanism for survival. Little imagination is necessary to envision how the rudimentary nature of striking could evolve into training activities for hunting and warfare, and, eventually, into an organized sport such as boxing. With any sport's development, however, the use of specialized equipment occurs, and the equipment, too, evolves over time. The literary and archaeological evidence, left by the ancients, provides much detail about boxing in antiquity, especially the type of equipment, particularly the glove (or lack thereof), that was used.[101]

A form of boxing known as *Pyx* (meaning 'with clenched fist') was introduced to the Olympics in 688 BCE where opponents were only allowed to punch. Other forms of attack such as grappling, biting and gouging were prohibited though

---

[101]Steven R. Murray, "Boxing Gloves of the Ancient World," *Journal of Combative Sport*, (July 2010). http://ejmas.com/jcs/2010jcs/jcsart_murray_1007.html.

it is hotly debated in the academic world if kicking was allowed. The object was to either knock out the opponent or force him to submit, which was indicated with a raised index finger. The fight would continue until a submission or knock out was achieved; in this particularly vicious version of the sport, there were no rounds and participants could keep punching even if their opponent was knocked to the floor.

A soft dirt pit known as a *skamma* was used to fight in and a referee oversaw the battle, carrying a switch to whip any fighter that broke the rules or stepped out of line. While these contests were brutal affairs, a fighter would still need high levels of training, skill and courage to make it in the boxing scene of ancient Greece...As well as being a sport and a gladiatorial contest, it was also seen as a training method for soldiers though safety equipment would have been used in this case to prevent injury during training. The boxing scene held an important role in Roman culture until around 400 CE, when Emperor Theodoric the Great banned it outright. As a Christian, he disapproved of the deaths and disfigurements it could cause, and of its use as a form of violent entertainment.[102]

When monitored and on a professional level, boxing is a skilled and highly disciplined sport that is a test of endurance and athletic prowess. Yet, there is a higher fight, and fight of righteousness that we are called to in this fallen world. It is a fight worth fighting for the good, for truth, for all that is holy, for the eternal souls of men and women. This chapter focuses on the fighting imagery that the apostle Paul uses in his exhortation to his son in the faith, Timothy, and to challenge him to assert his heart and soul in the heavenly fight for the gospel of Jesus Christ.

---

[102]Andrew Griffiths, "Boxing in the Ancient World," *The History of Fighting*. http://www.historyoffighting.com/boxing-in-the-ancient-world.php.

"Fight the good fight of the faith. Take hold of the eternal life to which you were called and about which you made the good confession in the presence of many witnesses" (1 Tim. 6:12).

The apostle Paul writing under divine inspiration, history says, from a Roman prison about AD 63-64, focused two entire letters on an apostolic mentorship with Timothy. Timothy, much seen through the letters of Paul and early church history, became the leading elder of the church in Ephesus. Paul was writing, in part, to shape a ministerial vision for Timothy, so that he would be best equipped to shepherd well the church placed under his care. The historical setting of Paul (2-3 years prior to his execution by the maniacal Roman Emperor Nero) would have been profound to Timothy himself.[103] Countless generations have benefitted and will benefit from this pastoral epistle, until the Lord returns.

---

[103] William Smith, *Smiths Bible Dictionary*, "Paul", "This epistle [2 Timothy], surely no unworthy utterance at such an age and in such an hour even of a St. Paul, brings us, it may well be presumed, close to the end of his life. For what remains, we have the concurrent testimony of ecclesiastical antiquity, that he was beheaded at Rome, about the same time that St. Peter was crucified there. The earliest allusion to the death of St. Paul is in that sentence from Clemens Romanus, ... which just fails of giving us any particulars upon which we can conclusively rely. The next authorities are those quoted by Eusebius in his H. E. ii. 25. Dionysius, bishop of Corinth (A. D. 170), says that Peter and Paul went to Italy and taught there together, and suffered martyrdom about the same time. This, like most of the statements relating to the death of St. Paul, is mixed up with the tradition, with which we are not here immediately concerned, of the work of St. Peter at Rome…Caius of Rome, supposed to be writing within the 2nd century, names the grave of St. Peter on the Vatican, and that of St. Paul on the Ostian way. Eusebius himself entirely adopts the tradition that St. Paul was beheaded under Nero at Rome. Amongst other early testimonies, we have that of Tertullian."

Paul sets forth various clear exhortations to the younger pastor, instructing Timothy to, "Keep a close watch on yourself and on the teaching. Persist in this, for by so doing you will save both yourself and your hearers" (1 Tim. 4:16). He states to Timothy: "This charge I entrust to you, Timothy, my child, in accordance with the prophecies previously made about you, that by them you may wage the good warfare, holding faith and a good conscience. By rejecting this, some have made shipwreck of their faith" (1 Tim. 1:18-19). Another example of his exhortations to Timothy is the focus of the sermon in 1 Timothy 6:12, to "Fight the good fight." One last example of the potent Pauline admonitions to Timothy is 1 Timothy 6:20-21, "O Timothy, guard the deposit entrusted to you. Avoid the irreverent babble and contradictions of what is falsely called 'knowledge,' for by professing it some have swerved from the faith. Grace be with you." Timothy was granted the sacred trust to be one of the stewards of the gospel mysteries in the early church, and Paul exhorts him to be faithful to the call.

Our text today is in the same spirit of the charge to Timothy from the apostle Paul just before his martyrdom. History strongly asserts that Paul had been beheaded by Nero about AD 67. First Timothy 6:12 then, a first line imperative by Paul to Timothy to "Fight the good fight of the Faith," is the focus of this chapter. Again, it was widely recognized that Paul was executed under the Roman persecutions shortly after 1 Timothy was written and very soon after 2 Timothy was written. These words of the senior Christian leader to his disciple and son in the faith would have remained with Timothy after the death of Paul. The treasures of 1 and 2 Timothy would have been his foundation for pastoral leadership as they have been for many generations of pastors since then.

Paul writes as a pastoral and missionary mentor to Timothy to encourage and guide him as an elder, teacher, and evangelist. The injunction to "Fight the good fight of the faith" will be considered here now to clarify why the fighting imagery is utilized again by Paul and what type of battle he is calling Timothy to. Two primary points

147

of the text to consider then are: 1) the reason behind the spiritual battle; and 2) the manner in which the fight must be fought.

The Reason Behind the Spiritual Battle

Beginning with a question is fitting: "What is the reason for the spiritual battle at hand?" Here in 1 Timothy one begins to understand the good battle that Paul was calling Timothy to fight, namely the battle of faith. Paul said to Timothy in 6:12 that God had called him firstly in his salvation and gave unto him eternal life. As well, in the context of the verse, we see that Timothy had made a profession of faith. Paul says, "You made the good confession in the presence of many witnesses." This "good confession" is believed to be a reference to the special moment in Timothy's life when he testified publically concerning his faith in the gospel. Just as Timothy had a public profession of faith it is foundational for every believer.

Going on, believers today need to proclaim Christ and then go on to fight the good fight of the faith. But then to ask, "What is the greater purpose of the battle?" This faith speaks of there being within every believer a battle that they have a personal responsibility to live out their faith profession. As believers then, there is a real war that they have the responsibility to defend the truth in. What is at stake to defend is not only that we live out the Christian faith daily in a devotional relationship with the Lord, but also in articulating and defending sound doctrine, theology, and standing for convictions on all ethical and moral issues. Also, included that we believe profoundly in the substance of our faith and that we embrace the certainty of truth, which our faith embodies.

Relating to this battle, Puritan Pastor Matthew Henry drew from 2 Corinthians 10:4-5, saying,

> The doctrines of the gospel and discipline of the church are the weapons of this warfare; and these are not carnal: outward force, therefore, is not the method of the gospel, but strong

persuasions, by the power of truth and the meekness of wisdom. A good argument this is against persecution for conscience' sake: conscience is accountable to God only; and people must be persuaded to God and their duty, not driven by force of arms. And so the weapons of our warfare are mighty, or very powerful; the evidence of truth is convincing and cogent.[104]

In other words, our weapons are not of the world or the flesh. Our battle, our war, is to believe and live out our faith. Referring again to 2 Corinthians 10:5, we must recognize that our battle exists against "arguments and every lofty opinion raised against the knowledge of God." And our struggle, Paul says, is to "take every thought captive to obey Christ." So then, we are to virtually attack each anti-Christian, unbiblical thought, emotion, or impulse that we experience.

This battle is primarily in the mind or heart. As Dr. George Zemek (former faculty at The Master's Seminary in Los Angeles, CA) refers to this inner man part of us, the "mission control center." However, the battle may have outside influences as the catalyst to the inner problem. For example, it may be television programs channeling ungodly philosophies into our family room (through innumerable soap operas, and series of teen drama episodes). The conflict may also be from false ideologies in the news or political commentaries that are aired into our home and family vehicle. It could be as well, required study classes or other anti-Christian philosophies that we find ourselves needing discernment for.

One illustration that Paul warned Timothy to protect his life against was the trap of the "love of money" and which could involve material possessions that would have been available to Timothy and other believers to be tempted by. In 1 Timothy 6:6-11 there is an implication that the desire to follow your sinful heart in love for

---

[104]Matthew Henry, *Matthew Henry's Commentary on the Whole Bible: Acts to Revelation*, (Peabody: Hendrickson Publishers, 1991), 511.

money or other things monetarily related that may seduce us (verse 9). Paul writes:

> But godliness with contentment is great gain, for we brought nothing into the world, and we cannot take anything out of the world. But if we have food and clothing, with these we will be content. But those who desire to be rich fall into temptation, into a snare, into many senseless and harmful desires that plunge people into ruin and destruction. For the love of money is a root of all kinds of evils. It is through this craving that some have wandered away from the faith and pierced themselves with many pangs. But as for you, O man of God, flee these things. Pursue righteousness, godliness, faith, love, steadfastness, gentleness.

This covetous lust for money and potential materialism is a sinful substitute for the real substance of a relationship with our God, through His Son Jesus Christ. If we choose the One, we will leave the other. To love Jesus is to abandon the love of money.

At times, many Christians have needed to defend their faith to a neighbor, relative, or friend. This defense of the Bible's truth should be considered as the battle we are talking about fighting this good fight of the faith. In such situations, it is imperative to recall Jesus Christ, His pain, His passion, His suffering, in the humiliation of Roman execution by crucifixion. We must remember that Christ died for each of us personally. That He suffered for *me*. We should reflect on His agony that He endured for us and persevere in the standing firm in the good fight.

If you have not begun to engage in this battle, it may be that reading this book filled with Holy Scripture will aid in sensing the reality of the spiritual war and your need to be saved. Today is the day to seek the salvation of the Lord, today is the day to call upon Him in your heart. "'Seek the LORD while he may be found; call upon him while he is near; let the wicked forsake his way, and the unrighteous man his thoughts; let him return to the LORD, that he may have compassion on him, and to our God, for he will abundantly pardon'" (Isa. 55:6-7).

The Manner in Which the Fight Must be Fought

Amazingly the heritage of warfighting in the United States is undergirded by a deep sense of ethical thinking with much traceable back to the Bible as its source. From the Center of Vision and Values at Grove City College is found an inspiring consideration of General George Washington:

> Both as commander-in-chief of the Continental Army and president, Washington worked to form an American character. Throughout the War for Independence, he expected both his officers and soldiers to act morally and 'display the character of republicans' appropriate to 'Christian Soldier[s]' who were defending their country's 'dearest Rights and Liberties.' Speaking to the nation's governors in 1783, Washington argued that Americans could 'establish or ruin their national Character forever.' As John Winthrop had done in his 1630 sermon 'A Model of Christian Charity,' Washington reminded his countrymen that 'the eyes of the whole World' were 'turned upon them.' Guided by the complementary principles of revelation and reason, Americans must fulfill their civic duties because they were 'actors on a most conspicuous Theatre ... peculiarly designated by Providence for the display of human greatness and felicity.'[105]

To Washington, and the early American patriots, to fight was simply not enough, but to fight with character and dignity for a just

---

[105]Gary S. Smith, "The Character of George Washington," *The Institute for Faith & Freedom.* http://www.visionandvalues.org/2010/03/the-character-of-george-washington/.

purpose was the greater standard to pursue. It is rare to find nobility and ethics underlying warfighting in world history. The United States, and certainly some other Western nations, would be rich in upholding at least a theoretical ethical framework for military aggression.

Another aspect that needs to be considered is certainly the question, "In what manner ought we to engage in this battle described in the New Testament?" Considering the wording of this verse again from the words of Paul to Timothy to "fight the good fight of the faith," it is good to consider more closely the word meaning. In the original Greek, the phrase, "Fight the good fight of the faith" (αγωνιζου τον καλον αγωνα της πιστεως) has the word mentioned previously and means literally, "to agonize." The phrase in a literal translation compels the believer to "agonize the good agony of the faith." The word group is very similar to our English word *struggle* or "to labor fervently" and it is used for contending athletically for a prize. Paul uses the imperative verb form here, commanding Timothy to "fight" or "struggle," literally "agonize."

This is a favorite saying or theme of Paul to use. Again it has relation to wording used to describe the Olympic Games. The sense is to fight, contend, or struggle to resist and defeat enemy forces who are opposed to the gospel or to opposed through actual anti-Christ efforts and ideologies. Paul uses the same word in 1 Corinthians 9:24-27, and the word is used in such a way as "to compete in the Olympic events":

> Do you not know that in a race all the runners run, but only one receives the prize? So run that you may obtain it. Every athlete *exercises* self-control in all things. They do it to receive a perishable wreath, but we an imperishable. So I do not run aimlessly; I do not box as one beating the air. But I discipline my body and keep it under control, lest after preaching to others I myself should be disqualified (1 Cor. 9:24-27, emphasis added).

The term here "exercises" (ESV), "striveth" (KJV), and "competes" (NASB, HCSB) speaks of this agonizing struggle, and is wonderfully illustrated by Paul with a reference to boxing (verse 26). Paul is emphasizing the reality of the fight, he is not just practicing, not merely shadow-boxing here (verse 26: "I do not box as one beating the air"), rather he is in the real fight, the actual fighting match for the gospel of Jesus Christ. Paul is stressing the weightiness and intensity of the fight here.

Friends, today are you running to obtain the spiritual prize in Jesus Christ?

Furthermore, the wording here (1 Tim. 6:12), indeed has the connotation of athletic struggle and the agony of the competition of the athletic event. Yet, also spoken of here is of such an interior or exterior battle, and the sense of continuing and maintaining the combative fight for the gospel truth. So this good fight of faith then always is ongoing, and it has no end this side of heaven. At the end of his life, Paul writes:

For I am already being poured out as a drink offering, and the time of my departure has come. I have fought the good fight, I have finished the race, I have kept the faith. Henceforth there is laid up for me the crown of righteousness, which the Lord, the righteous judge, will award to me on that day, and not only to me but also to all who have loved his appearing (2 Tim. 4:6-8).

The context of 2 Timothy, as alluded to earlier, is Paul under sentence of death by Rome. Most likely he was awaiting his execution by beheading. Yet he writes, faith-filled and valiant. He had fought the good fight, finished the race, and kept the faith. He had his heart fixed on heaven and the wonderful entrance he would enjoy there, and an entrance that awaits all who know the Lord.

153

Questions for Spiritual Formation:

1. According to the text at hand, what is the reason for the spiritual battle? "Fight the good fight of the faith. Take hold of the eternal life to which you were called and about which you made the good confession in the presence of many witnesses" (1 Tim. 6:12).

2. How may you evaluate yourself to determine if you are running to obtain the spiritual prize in Jesus Christ?

3. How is the Christian expected to manage this inner man part of him or her, the "mission control center"? How can ungodly desires take root in the mind of the genuine Christian?

4. How does the following text apply to the chapter: "But godliness with contentment is great gain, for we brought nothing into the world, and we cannot take anything out of the world. But if we have food and clothing, with these we will be content" (1 Timothy 6:6-8).

Who is on the Lord's side?
by Frances Ridley Havergal

Who is on the Lord's side?
Who will serve the King?
Who will be His helpers,
Other lives to bring?
Who will leave the world's side?
Who will face the foe?
Who is on the Lord's side?
Who for Him will go?

Chorus:
By Thy grand redemption,
By Thy grace divine,
We are on the Lord's side;
Savior, we are Thine.

Not for weight of glory,
Not for crown and palm,
Enter we the army,
Raise the warrior psalm;
But for love that claimeth
Lives for whom He died;
He whom Jesus nameth
Must be on His side.

Jesus, Thou hast bought us,
Not with gold or gem,
But with Thine own life-blood,
For Thy diadem;
With Thy blessing filling
Each who comes to Thee,
Thou hast made us willing,
Thou hast made us free.

Fierce may be the conflict,
Strong may be the foe,
But the King's own army
None can overthrow.
Round His standard ranging
Victory is secure,
For His truth unchanging
Makes the triumph sure.

Chosen to be soldiers
In an alien land:
Chosen, called, and faithful,
For our Captain's band;
In the service royal
Let us not grow cold;
Let us be right loyal,
Noble, true, and bold.[106]

---

[106]Frances Ridley Havergal, *Who is on the Lord's Side* (Public Domain, 1877).

Chapter 12

Apocalyptic Readiness
for the Christian

On April 16th, 1775, The Patriot, Paul Revere began to gather tips that a raid was planned for the city of Concord in the coming days. In fact, it is speculated that these tips came from General Gage's wife, an American who may have been sympathetic to the plight of her countrymen. With this intelligence, Revere began making plans to alert the surrounding countryside by horseback that the redcoats would indeed be arriving to ransack their military supplies.

There were two routes that the British soldiers could take: by land through the Boston Neck and by sea across the Charles River. Paul Revere arranged to have a signal lit in the Old North Church – one lantern if the British were coming by land and two lanterns if they were coming by sea – and began to make preparations for his ride to alert the local militias and citizens about the impending attack.

On April 18th, 1775, 700 British soldiers under the command of Lieutenant Colonel Francis Smith gathered on Boston Common and boarded ships to raid Concord. These soldiers included eight companies of grenadiers, or soldiers who stood on the frontlines and heaved grenades at the enemy, and eight companies of light infantry.

During this time, Paul Revere, along with two other riders, William Dawes and Samuel Prescott, began their nighttime rides to rouse the minutemen and warn citizens of an attack. Revere rode to Lexington, where Samuel Adams and John Hancock were staying en route to the Second Continental Congress, and managed to persuade Adams and Hancock to leave the city for their safety as they faced possible arrest. Revere was later captured, but fortunately for the Patriots, this occurred after the news of a British attack had already been conveyed.[107]

"Therefore, preparing your minds for action, and being sober-minded, set your hope fully on the grace that will be brought to you at the revelation of Jesus Christ" (1 Peter 1:13).

The apostle Peter, a leader amongst the apostles, wrote in extreme times of persecution, not many years before he was executed by the Romans, and gained the crown of martyrdom that almost every other apostle experienced as well as countless others throughout church history. As the Christians that Peter was writing to would have understood, 1:3 states, that God "according to His great mercy" had caused them "to be born again" to a new and "living hope through the resurrection of Jesus Christ from the dead." Of course, they had been "grieved by various trials" (verse 6), which living under the diabolical reign of the Roman Emperor Nero had brought them.

They would have known and were reminded by the writing of 1 Peter that they had an extraordinary spiritual "inheritance...reserved in heaven." In light of this powerful salvation of their souls (verse 9), and things into which angels desired to observe (verse 12), they were to live with a type of readiness. This type of battlefield

---

[107]Boston Tea Party, "Paul Revere's Ride: The Patriots Prepare for Battle," *Boston Tea Party Ships & Museum.* https://www.bostonteapartyship.com/paul-reveres-ride.

mentality was to remain with them as they pursued holiness in a perverse generation in light of the impending judgment of God (2:12). One passage shows Peter desiring to help the saints be reminded of these realities is 4:3-5. They were saved from such things, and the pagans continue in such sinfulness, in light of the impending wrath of God.

Thus, Peter charges the church to engage in adopting this mindset model of which 1:13 prescribes three characteristics of this apocalyptic readiness that was needed in the intense period of persecution in the first few hundred years of the Christian church. It is certainly needed today as we wait the imminent return of Jesus Christ. So almost 2,000 years later, these same instructions are pertinent for all believers in this godless age. The three aspects of this readiness mindset that Peter proposes for us are:

1) Gird your minds for action
2) Keep sober in spirit
3) Focus your hope.

Gird Your Minds for Action

In light of the situation, Peter called for the early Christians to gird their minds for action, i.e., to be preparing their minds for action. This is the appropriate battlefield cry today for all believers. In the climate of the anti-Christ spirit of their times, the early church lived out their faith in the living God. Today, likewise, all Christians must gain a serious perspective, a wartime posture for preparedness.

The wording "Gird your minds for action" and which the KJV translates "Gird up the loins of your mind" has the exact application and meaning as the KJV implicates. The KJV translation brings out the metaphor of the text, i.e., "the loins of the mind." This prepared state of mind speaks literally of keeping the mind held in a state of constant preparation. The aspect of girding up your loins comes from the Old Testament instruction for the Israelites as they were preparing for Passover.

Remember, the Passover dinner was to be eaten when the angel of death was about to pass over the homes of the Hebrew families in Goshen:

> The LORD said to Moses and Aaron in the land of Egypt, 'This month shall be for you the beginning of months. It shall be the first month of the year for you. Tell all the congregation of Israel that on the tenth day of this month every man shall take a lamb according to their fathers' houses, a lamb for a household…You may take it from the sheep or from the goats, and you shall keep it until the fourteenth day of this month, when the whole assembly of the congregation of Israel shall kill their lambs at twilight. Then they shall take some of the blood and put it on the two doorposts and the lintel of the houses in which they eat it…They shall eat the flesh that night, roasted on the fire; with unleavened bread and bitter herbs they shall eat it…<u>In this manner you shall eat it: with your belt fastened, your sandals on your feet, and your staff in your hand</u>. And you shall eat it in haste. It is the LORD's Passover. For I will pass through the land of Egypt that night, and I will strike all the firstborn in the land of Egypt, both man and beast; and on all the gods of Egypt I will execute judgments: I am the LORD. The blood shall be a sign for you, on the houses where you are. And when I see the blood, I will pass over you, and no plague will befall you to destroy you, when I strike the land of Egypt. (Ex. 12:1-14, emphasis added).

They were to prepare their lives and families for the event by designating their homes through faith. This designation was done by applying a young lamb's blood to the doorposts outside their front doors. Then they were to boil the lamb and eat it as the family awaited the deliverance of God from Egypt. Notice as well, they had instruction on how to eat it, they were to eat with their belts fastened. (The KJV states, "With [their] loins girded.") Here is reflected the ancient Eastern cultural attire for a man, which was a long flowing garment, and requirements for rapid movement. When they needed to move quickly, perhaps running, they would "gird their loins" for quick movement. This was the lifting up of one corner of the garment and tucking it into the belt. This is found in other texts as well, and would have had a strong visual significance for the Israelites. (1 Kings 18:46; 2 Kings 4:29; 2 Kings 9:1)

Again, this was a metaphor for being prepared, taken from the Eastern practice of tucking their gown into their belt. One Bible dictionary explains it as, "a metaphor derived from the practice of the Orientals, who in order to be unimpeded in their movements were accustomed, when starting a journey or engaging in any work, to bind their long flowing garments closely around their bodies and fastened them with a leather belt."[108] This was a call by Peter, in 1 Peter 1:13, to alertness in the Christian life.

Here Peter applies this to the mind, having mental preparedness and alertness for action. Bible teachers believe this is directly in connection with the end of the verse: "Set your hope fully on the grace that will be brought to you at the revelation of Jesus Christ." Calvin comments about this illustration of girding or preparing the mind:

> It is a similitude taken from an ancient custom; for when they had long garments, they could not make a journey, nor conveniently do any work, without being girded up. Hence these expressions, to gird up one's-self for a work or an undertaking. He then bids them to remove all impediments, that being set at liberty they might go on to God... And he intimates that our minds are held entangled by the passing cares of the world and by vain desires, so that they rise not upward to God. Whosoever, then, really wishes to have this hope, let

---

[108] *Thayer's Greek definitions*, ἀναζώννυμι.

him learn in the first place to disentangle himself from the world, and gird up his mind that it may not turn aside to vain affections.[109]

This nature of mental preparedness has a direct correlation to the expectancy of the return of Christ.

Keep Sober in Spirit

In the second part of the verse, Peter calls for the early saints to be "sober in spirit." Literally the term means "to be free from the influence of intoxicants," but in this context with the anticipation of the return of Christ it takes on the meaning of "watchfulness." In other words, this figurative use of the word means "clarity of mind," yet with specific reference to the anticipation of the Second Coming of the Lord Jesus.

This sobriety of the spirit is then the frame of mind that God is calling believers to the New Testament context. They are to have a heightened awareness of the return of Jesus to the world. Peter, thus, uses the word again referring to the end of the age, but for the purpose of prayer, "The end of all things is at hand; therefore, be self-controlled and sober-minded for the sake of your prayers" (1 Peter 4:7). The prayer warrior was to be sober in mind in such difficult times as they were living in, and certainly would apply to many circumstances today for those who take a stand in the culture for the truth of the Bible.

At the time of this writing (2017), as a U.S. Army Chaplain, I was stationed along with my wife and 5 children in beautiful Hawaii. As I was studying, I became greatly aware of the surrounding tranquility and loveliness of Hawaii and I immediately thought this verse felt almost other worldly. This verse and the wider context of 1 Peter seems distant from the peacefulness of the ocean breeze here and the sound of the waves on western Oahu early in the morning

---

[109]Calvin, *The Catholic Epistles*, 44-45.

and late in the evening. Some readers of this book may relate to the present comfort of general safety and serenity. The harshness of the New Testament climate of danger and   violent persecution seemed very remote in my current situation. Yet, it is clear that Christians are experiencing such violent opposition in various places in our world today.

Nevertheless, believers everywhere must remain with a sense of alertness and not allow the comforts of life and freedom from immediate harm to allure them from the sweetness of the crucified and risen Lord Jesus. The blessings of daily life must be appreciated as evidences of divine mercy, being also of grace from our loving God in the present. The believer must guard against idols that form and threaten to eclipse the character of God in our thoughts. These niceties and present state of the kindness of God should not dull us in light of the responsibilities God has given to us, to remain alert, to gird up the loins of our minds, to be sober in spirit, as well as to fix our hope on the grace to be brought to us when Jesus returns. Again Peter uses the term in a warning to the believers in 1 Peter 5:8-9: "Be sober-minded; be watchful. Your adversary the devil prowls around like a roaring lion, seeking someone to devour. Resist him, firm in your faith, knowing that the same kinds of suffering are being experienced by your brotherhood throughout the world."

Here Peter speaks of a mental preparedness, not to be ignorant of the reality of the ways of Satan in the world. As well, there is a sense of self-discipline, or self-control, as the NIV translates it. Thayer's Greek dictionary defines this term "to be sober, to be calm and collected in spirit."[110] This is stated as well in 5:8 as an imperative by Peter; it is a command for the believers to follow from the good apostle. This is a pastoral command, exhorting believers to beware of the devil and to replicate this conduct of being self-controlled, prepared in mind, and highly conscious of the forthcoming return of Jesus Christ.

---

[110]*Thayer's Greek Definitions*, 1 Pet. 5:8, νηψατε.

Focus Your Hope

This aspect and the last portion of the text of 1 Peter 1:13 reads, "Set your hope fully on the grace that will be brought to you at the revelation of Jesus Christ." Much could be said here, but let us focus on key details. Commentators on 1 Peter have said this portion is the central idea of the verse. One could summarize the verse and this chapter by saying, "While you are fixing your hope on the grace to be brought to you at the return of Christ, gird your mind for action and keep sober in spirit."

To consider this last portion to "set your hope fully on the grace that will be brought to you at the revelation of Jesus Christ," let me point out something that the verse does not say. Peter says nothing of worrying about *when* Jesus will return. Rather this verse, and many others related to the return of Christ to the world, focuses on the imminence—which is the perspective that the second advent of Jesus could happen soon. Therefore, we should be concerning ourselves with our attitude and outlook to be prepared in mind and sober spirited.

One can look at what this action is, namely to fixate one's hope on something. It is also to consider the object of your *hope*, namely upon the undeserved grace of God that will be brought to you when Jesus returns. *Hope* in the pages of the Bible is filled with great confidence, and a "confident expectation." The author of Hebrews, in 11:1 speaks of things "hoped for" spiritually speaking and of that hoped for thing, "faith is the assurance," and that faith is also the "conviction of things not yet seen." Protestant reformers spoke of an inner witness of the Holy Spirit, the hope the believer has is a faith-filled and comfortably confident hope.

The apostle Paul also speaks of this great hope, and he focuses on the eternal plan of God in Romans 8:24-25, where he writes, "For in this hope we were saved. Now hope that is seen is not hope. For who hopes for what he sees? But if we hope for what we do not see, we wait for it with patience." Here he speaks of a real and confident hope in what one cannot see. In Romans 15:13, Paul writes as a benediction, "May the God of hope fill you with all joy and peace in believing, so that by the power of the Holy Spirit you may abound in hope." Notice, he states that believers abound in hope by the power of the Holy Spirit (literally, we "overflow in hope" or "superabound" in such hope).

As an illustration of hope, consider an example of lesser profundity. If my son Abraham, when he was a younger child, came to me late at night or early in the morning and said he was thirsty and asked if I would help him go downstairs to get a glass of water. If I said, "Just a minute, I'm finishing up something I am reading," he would know he could have a sure confident hope that I would help him in a few minutes. Since I have loved him and often helped him with simple tasks in life that may be easier for me than for him, he would have known that I generally never break a promise without a very important reason. He would not immediately become filled with despair because he would be very confident that I would do what I have said, I would help him within a few minutes. He has a basic trustful assurance that my promise was and is real. The believer should have perhaps even a greater confident hope that what our heavenly Father has said will absolutely happen, He will keep his word.

Of course, it can be seen in what Peter has written in 1:13 that the great object of our hope that will be bestowed upon the saints when Jesus returns is this "grace of God." To be certain, this underserved grace will be reserved for the elect alone, those who have secured their "calling and election" through assuring that the qualities of godliness are progressing in their lives (2 Peter 1:10). The question may be asked further here, "What is the grace of God to be brought to us?" This grace, Bible teachers have written, refers to an emphasis of all the great heavenly blessings that are ours in Christ.

Peter instructed believers of a grace and peace from God that he desired for them all. As well, Peter spoke further of the blessing of the grace that is for the Christian by the coming and suffering of

Christ in His humanity. That is the grace of which the prophets contemplated and of that which was preached in Peter's day (down to today) in the message of the gospel.

As well, amazingly this grace that is to be brought to all believers is actually a grace that is literally on its way (due to the present passive participle of the grace being brought). It is a present and passive grace, and grace is always passive, it is something being done for us underserving saved sinners. What a grace, a wonderful grace that we currently have in Christ, in our redemption, in the total forgiveness of God, in our justification and eternal life. Yet amazingly, the future culmination of this grace-gift to all believers is going to be when every eye will see Him (Rev. 1:7). The day is coming; let us all be alert, prepared in mind, sober-minded, and setting our hope on Him! The apostle Peter warns:

> This is now the second letter that I am writing to you, beloved. In both of them I am stirring up your sincere mind by way of reminder, that you should remember the predictions of the holy prophets and the commandment of the Lord and Savior through your apostles, knowing this first of all, that scoffers will come in the last days with scoffing, following their own sinful desires. They will say, "Where is the promise of his coming? For ever since the fathers fell asleep, all things are continuing as they were from the beginning of creation." For they deliberately overlook this fact, that the heavens existed long ago, and the earth was formed out of water and through water by the word of God, and that by means of these the world that then existed was deluged with water and perished. But by the same word the heavens and earth that now exist are stored up for fire, being kept until the day of judgment and destruction of the ungodly. (2 Peter 3:1-7).

The day of judgment and wrath is coming for the unbeliever and the believer is to be disciplined in anticipation, alert and prepared to meet him.

Questions for Spiritual Formation:

1. What is the significance of the instruction to "Gird your minds for action" and which the KJV translates "Gird up the loins of your mind"?

2. In light of ten periods of persecution under the Roman era that the early Christians felt, what further implications can be considered in the imperative to watchfulness in the "Be sober in spirit" teaching by Peter?

3. How can an eschatological mindedness—a mindfulness that the return of Jesus Christ is closely upon the world—impact our faith and day-to-day living?

4. Why is it more important to contemplate the general imminent nature to the Lord Jesus's return than try to narrow down and teach political events and natural disasters in light of eschatology prophecies?

Originally the classic hymn "Soldiers of Christ, Arise" had a few more verses than traditionally sung, most are added below. They are wonderful to contemplate and reflect much of Paul's writings on the spiritual armor. Charles Wesley (1707-1788) has packed much truth and passion into this time-honored hymn, and truly historical theme.

Soldiers of Christ, Arise

Soldiers of Christ, arise, and put your armor on,
Strong in the strength which God supplies through His eternal Son.
Strong in the Lord of hosts, and in His mighty power,
Who in the strength of Jesus trusts is more than conqueror.

Stand then in His great might, with all His strength endued,
But take, to arm you for the fight, the panoply of God;
That, having all things done, and all your conflicts passed,
Ye may o'er come through Christ alone and stand entire at last.

Stand then against your foes, in close and firm array;
Legions of wily fiends oppose throughout the evil day.
But meet the sons of night, and mock their vain design,
Armed in the arms of heavenly light, of righteousness divine.

Leave no unguarded place, no weakness of the soul,
Take every virtue, every grace, and fortify the whole;
Indissolubly joined, to battle all proceed;
But arm yourselves with all the mind that was in Christ, your Head.

But, above all, lay hold on faith's victorious shield;
Armed with that adamant and gold, be sure to win the field:
If faith surround your heart, Satan shall be subdued,
Repelled his every fiery dart, and quenched with Jesu's blood.

Jesus hath died for you! What can His love withstand?
Believe, hold fast your shield, and who shall pluck you from His hand?

Believe that Jesus reigns; all power to Him is giv'n:
Believe, till freed from sin's remains; believe yourselves to Heav'n.

To keep your armor bright, attend with constant care,
Still walking in your Captain's sight, and watching unto prayer.
Ready for all alarms, steadfastly set your face,
And always exercise your arms, and use your every grace.

Pray without ceasing, pray, your Captain gives the word;
His summons cheerfully obey and call upon the Lord;
To God your every want in instant prayer display,
Pray always; pray and never faint; pray, without ceasing, pray!

From strength to strength go on, wrestle and fight and pray,
Tread all the powers of darkness down and win the well fought day;
Still let the Spirit cry in all His soldiers, "Come!"
Till Christ the Lord descends from high and takes the conquerors
home.[111]

---

[111]Charles Wesley, *Soldiers of Christ Arise* (Public Domain, 1749).

Chapter 13

The Nature of the Believer's Weapons

(Excerpt of the *Pilgrim's Progress* by John Bunyan)

But now, in this Valley of Humiliation, poor CHRISTIAN was hard put to it; for he had gone but a little way, before he espied a foul fiend coming over the field to meet with him; his name was APOLLYON. Then did CHRISTIAN begin to be afraid, and to cast in his mind whether to go back or to stand his ground. But he considered again, that he had no armour for his back, and therefore thought that to turn the back to him might give him greater advantage with ease to pierce him with his darts; therefore, he resolved to venture, and stand his ground. For, thought he, had I no more in mine eye than the saving of my life, it would be the best way to stand.

So he went on, and APOLLYON met him. Now the monster was hideous to behold; he was clothed with scales like a fish (and they are his pride); he had wings like a dragon; feet like a bear; and out of his belly came fire and smoke; and his mouth was as the mouth of a lion. When he was come up to CHRISTIAN, he beheld him with a disdainful countenance, and thus began to question with him:

Apollyon. Whence come you, and whither are you bound?

Chr. I am come from the city of Destruction, which is the place of all evil, and am going to the City of Zion.

Apol. By this I perceive thou art one of my subjects; for all that country is mine, and I am the prince and god of it. How is it, then, that thou hast run away from thy king? Were it not that I hope thou mayest do me more service, I would strike thee   now   at   one   blow   to   the   ground.

Chr. I was born indeed in your dominions; but your service was hard, and your wages such as a man could not live on, for the wages of sin is death; therefore, when I was come to years, I did as other prudent persons do, look out, if perhaps I might mend myself.

Apol. There is no prince that will thus lightly lose his subjects; neither will I as yet lose thee. But since thou complainest of thy service and wages, be content to go back; what our country will afford I do here promise to give thee.

Chr. But I have let myself to another, even to the king of princes; and how can I with fairness go back with thee? ....

Apol. Thou didst faint at first setting out, when thou wast almost choked in the Gulf of Despond; thou didst attempt wrong ways to be rid of thy burden, whereas thou shouldst have stayed till thy Prince had taken it off; thou didst sinfully sleep and lose thy choice thing; thou wast also almost persuaded to go back at the sight of the lions; and when thou talkest of thy journey, and of what thou hast heard and seen, thou art inwardly desirous of vain-glory in all that thou sayest or doest.

Chr. All this is true; and much more which thou hast left out: but the Prince whom I serve and honour is merciful and ready to forgive. But besides, these infirmities possessed me in thy country; for there I sucked them in, and I have groaned under them, been sorry for them, and have obtained pardon of my Prince.

Apol. Then APOLLYON broke out into a grievous rage, saying, "I am an enemy to this Prince: I hate his person, his laws, and people: I am come out on purpose to withstand thee."

Chr. APOLLYON, beware what you do; for I am in the King's highway, the way of holiness: therefore take heed to yourself!

Apol. Then APOLLYON straddled quite over the whole breadth of the way, and said, "I am void of fear in this matter: prepare thyself to die! for I swear by my infernal den that thou shalt go no farther; here will I spill thy soul." And with that he threw a flaming dart at his breast; but CHRISTIAN had a shield in his hand, with which he caught it, and so prevented the danger of that. Then did CHRISTIAN draw, for he saw 't was time to bestir him; and APOLLYON as fast made at him, throwing darts as thick as hail; by the which, notwithstanding all that CHRISTIAN could do to avoid it, APOLLYON wounded him in his head, his hand, and foot. This made CHRISTIAN give a little back; APOLLYON therefore followed his work furiously, and CHRISTIAN again took courage, and resisted as manfully as he could. This sore combat lasted for above half a day, even till CHRISTIAN was almost quite spent. For you must know that CHRISTIAN, by reason of his wounds, grew weaker and weaker.

Then APOLLYON, espying his opportunity, began to gather up close to CHRISTIAN, and wrestling with him, gave him a dreadful fall: and with that, CHRISTIAN'S sword flew out of his hand. Then said APOLLYON, "I am sure of thee now"; and with that he had almost pressed him to death, so that CHRISTIAN began to despair of life. But as God would have it, while APOLLYON was fetching his last blow, thereby to make a full end of this good man, CHRISTIAN nimbly reached out his hand for his sword, and caught it, saying, "Rejoice not against me, O mine enemy; when I fall, I shall

172

arise"(Micah 7:8), and with that, gave him a deadly thrust, which made him give back, as one that had received his mortal wound. CHRISTIAN perceiving that, made at him again, saying, "Nay, in all these things we are more than conquerors, through him that loved us".

And with that, APOLLYON spread forth his dragon's wings, and sped him away, that CHRISTIAN for a season saw him no more. In this combat no man can imagine, unless he had seen and heard as I did, what yelling and hideous roaring APOLLYON made all the time of the fight – he spake like a dragon; and, on the other side, what sighs and groans burst from CHRISTIAN'S heart. I never saw him all the while give so much as one pleasant look, till he perceived he had wounded APOLLYON with his two edged sword, then, indeed, he did smile, and look upward; but 'twas the dreadfullest sight that ever I saw! when the battle was over, CHRISTIAN said, "I will here give thanks to him that hath delivered me out of the mouth of the lion..."[112]

....

For though we walk in the flesh, we are not waging war according to the flesh. For the weapons of our warfare are not of the flesh but have divine power to destroy strongholds. We destroy arguments and every lofty opinion raised against the knowledge of God, and take every thought captive to obey Christ (2 Cor. 10:3-5).

Though termed the Nature of the Believer's Weapons, this chapter could well be titled, "The Spiritual Battle for Your Mind." In 2 Corinthians, the apostle Paul and his missionary companions had endured much affliction and difficulty—and had considered all

---

[112]John Bunyan, *The Pilgrim's Progress*, (Project Gutenberg. Public Domain), https://www.gutenberg.org/files/39452/39452-h/39452-h.htm. 75-81.

of their sufferings a part of the privilege to be representatives of the gospel. Paul had experienced much with the Corinthians and there is a fatherly and gracious tone in the epistle.

In 2 Corinthians 3 we read that Paul, in his fatherly tone, did not demand that the Corinthians obey his apostolic authority, but instead he described to them and explained that they are a spiritual letter in his and his missionary companions' hearts (3:2). Paul had been teaching Corinthians to trust their leaders (including himself). In the letter, Paul has written a leadership manual that Christians should use today. It is a type of pastoral instruction guide. Second Corinthians also contains an apostolic model for the church of our age. In other words, 2 Corinthians demonstrates the heart of an apostle who, in his time, should have been more widely respected, and his authority received, yet churches and individuals at times did not treat him or receive him as apostolic leadership ought to have been.

Chapter 10 of 2 Corinthians includes a portion concerning the spiritual weapons, which are also available for the present war that is being waged today against God. The NIV translates verse 4, "The weapons we fight with are not the weapons of the world." In his own spiritual war, Paul needed to present a defense for his apostolic ministerial office and of the role of biblical truth.

Paul was often attacked by false prophets that had invaded the church in Corinth. Paul as the spiritual father of the Corinthian Church had a great sense and perspective of his personal responsibility to protect the flock. In light of the spiritual war at the time in Corinth, Paul asserted two aspects in 10:5 of the spiritual war we are fighting. One aspect is to destroy false strongholds of thinking. The second is to honor God with our own thought life. Let's focus on these a bit more.

To Destroy False Strongholds of Thinking

It is necessary to consider more of the context in our passage. Think of the situation that Paul is defending by describing that we do not fight in the spiritual war "according to our flesh" or "not as

174

the world does," but he writes, "For the weapons of our warfare are not of the flesh but have divine power to destroy strongholds" (2 Cor. 10:4). So, he is saying metaphorically (using a battlefield illustration) that there are weapons—like military weapons, but specifically applied to the Christian life. Paul used the same word in the same metaphorical sense in Romans 13:12 that teaches we need to utilize "the armor of light." Here the putting on of the armor of light is described identically as putting on Christ: The night is far gone; the day is at hand. So then let us cast off the works of darkness and put on the armor of light...put on the Lord Jesus Christ and make no provision for the flesh (Rom. 13:12, 14).

Similarly, Paul described himself as using, in the spiritual conflict at hand, *the weapons of righteousness.* The context is provided to get the sense of how much he saw that the battle was relentlessly surrounding them at all times:

> As servants of God, we commend ourselves in every way: by great endurance, in afflictions, hardships, calamities, beatings, imprisonments, riots, labors, sleepless nights, hunger; by purity, knowledge, patience, kindness, the Holy Spirit, genuine love; by truthful speech, and the power of God; *with the weapons of righteousness* for the right hand and for the left; through honor and dishonor, through slander and praise. We are treated as impostors, and yet are true; as unknown, and yet well known; as dying, and behold, we live; as punished, and yet not killed; as sorrowful, yet always rejoicing; as poor, yet making many rich; as having nothing, yet possessing everything (2 Cor. 6:4-10, emphasis added).

It is imperative that the Christian life be engaged in active spiritual conflict, a battle that is raging.

Henceforth, in relation to these weapons of the spiritual war, we read in verse four of 2 Corinthians 10 that they are "divinely powerful for the destruction of fortresses" (NASB) or that they "have divine power to destroy strongholds" (ESV). These fortresses or strongholds facing the believer are described as well by Paul in verse 5 as "arguments and every lofty opinion raised against the knowledge of God" or, as the NASB states, are "speculations and every lofty thing raised up against the knowledge of God." This is a war of ideas and philosophies raised against the Kingdom of God. The church faces these wicked ideologies every day in our society, in the news, in the media, the internet, movies, music, books, and tragically even in churches.

Paul is explaining that these ideologies are based on evil concepts and false teachings. He says they are conquered by weapons that are available to us in Christ. So then, as the people of God, we are to have tremendous confidence that our weapons in Christ are sufficient for the battle. In such destruction of ideological fortresses—or strongholds that are waging war against the Kingdom of God—Paul says that we must destroy the speculations or arguments and everything raised up against God in this fallen world. Additionally, these speculations speak of things we encounter every day in the world; these are ideas and opinions that aggressively oppose the Bible and the truth of God (verse 5).

Thus we are instructed to destroy, or literally "knock down" these false ideas or ungodly ways of thinking. So these teachings, philosophies, heresies, "doctrines ("teachings," ESV) of demons" (1 Tim. 4:1) are confronted in the work of spiritual warfare. Such false teachings are these mentioned "fortresses" or "strongholds" that wage war against the ways of the Lord. Again, these are concepts, notions, perceptions that contradict the heaven-sent truth of God.

One pastor that I have been mentored and shepherded by through my seminary education and have listened to preaching from in person and through media for over 25 years has been Dr. John MacArthur. He writes that:

> The fortresses mentioned here are not demons but ideologies. The idea that spiritual warfare includes direct confrontation with demons is foreign to Scripture...the battle is rather with the false ideologies of men and demons propagate so that the

world believes them. Doomed souls are inside their fortresses of ideas, which become their prisons and eventually their tombs-unless they are delivered from them by belief in the truth.[113]

Believer, *what ideologies are currently controlling your thought life?*

The pastor I just quoted is right, we need to live like the apostle Peter writes: "But in your hearts honor Christ the Lord as holy, always being prepared to make a defense to anyone who asks you for a reason for the hope that is in you; yet do it with gentleness and respect" (1 Peter 3:15). The modern-day church needs to be on alert, always prepared. In the text focused on in this chapter—2 Corinthians 10:5—we read of the corrupted speculations of man, and "every lofty opinion raised against the knowledge of God."

One illustration from the early Christian church is Acts 17:22-31 where Paul was physically led by the men of Athens to present to them this message:

So Paul, standing in the midst of the Areopagus, said: "Men of Athens, I perceive that in every way you are very religious. For as I passed along and observed the objects of your worship, I found also an altar with this inscription, 'To the unknown god.' What therefore you worship as unknown, this I proclaim to you. The God who made the world and everything in it, being Lord of heaven and earth, does not live in temples made by man, nor is he served by human hands, as though he needed anything, since he himself gives to all mankind life and breath and everything. And he made from one man every nation of mankind to live on all the face of the

---

[113]John MacArthur, *The MacArthur New Testament Commentary 2 Corinthians,* (Chicago: Moody Publishers, 2003), 329.

earth, having determined allotted periods and the boundaries of their dwelling place, that they should seek God, and perhaps feel their way toward him and find him. Yet he is actually not far from each one of us, for 'In him we live and move and have our being'; as even some of your own poets have said, 'For we are indeed his offspring.' Being then God's offspring, we ought not to think that the divine being is like gold or silver or stone, an image formed by the art and imagination of man. The times of ignorance God overlooked, but now he commands all people everywhere to repent, because he has fixed a day on which he will judge the world in righteousness by a man whom he has appointed; and of this he has given assurance to all by raising him from the dead.

Just prior to this text Paul says he discussed or "was reasoning" in the synagogue "and in the marketplace every day" (verse 17). There were philosophers who were very religious, they worshipped an unknown God in ignorance.

Paul, in Acts 17 in Athens, Greece, preached and explained God as Creator, and the God who is not "like gold or silver or stone" (verse 29). Paul had defended the truth and confronted the speculations of the Greek philosophers and Jews in the synagogues. Also, after his message he saw a bit of the harvest that the Lord had prepared; some mocked him, some were interested to hear more about the gospel, and some actually became converted by the message he preached to them (verses 32-34). Here we see that Paul had preached against the (ideological) fortresses of the Greek philosophers and that God blessed His Word (which "never returns void") and various people believed and were saved.

To Honor God with Our Own Thought Life

Looking on to the second point in this chapter and second half of the text, we began in 2 Corinthians 10:5, "Take every thought captive to obey Christ." Paul here teaches something more referring to "the weapons" of our spiritual warfare. This portion could also be entitled, "Truth on the guidance of the mind." Paul is saying in this line of Scripture, on one hand, his apostolic struggle included the work of taking every thought captive as a follower of Christ. However, as Christians, our responsibility is to actively "take every thought captive to the obedience of Christ."

Let it be considered here the idea of taking one's thoughts captive that exist in the mind, thoughts that are contrary to the sound words of Scripture. The word, in the verb phrase in English, "*taking captive*" (in the taking captive of ungodly thoughts), has the sense "to incarcerate or take prisoner," and another Bible dictionary states the verb means to be "conquered," or even taken *captive* by sword, to be *captive*. The verb used here is also used by Luke in Luke 4:18, in the words of Jesus concerning His work of proclaiming liberty to the captives, used of those taken captive by the devil. As well, that which is needed to be taken captive is exclusively our private thought life. The believer must take a vigilant posture to disentangle himself from false ideologies and must dismantle the arguments and opinions asserted in opposition to the knowledge of God.

That is right because outside of Jesus Christ there exists many wordly lies and false teachings and we need to live in the perspective of spiritual warfare, and progressively so each day. In 10:5 of 2 Corinthians, the word *thought* speaks of these lies against God. The word here means "to perceive" and bears the literal sense of a thought or concept of the mind. Such thinking is mentioned earlier in 4:4, where the unbelievers are described as having such thoughts are blind. Paul says, "In their case the god of this world has blinded the minds of the unbelievers, to keep them from seeing the light of the gospel of the glory of Christ, who is the image of God" (2 Cor. 4:4).

In wrapping up this chapter there is the reminder to take all captive under "the obedience of Christ." This is key, we cannot finish without this. Literally, the phrase means, "to the complete obedience that is required by Christ," but it is also used generally of the relationship between a slave and his master. Conceptually it is used also of the bond between God the Son and God the Father. The Son walked in humble submission to the Father only doing what the Father desired or permitted Him to do. So Jesus said to them, "Truly, truly, I say to you, the Son can do nothing of his own accord, but only what he sees the Father doing. For whatever the Father does, that the Son does likewise (John 5:19).

It may be concluded then, that all Christ-followers need to continue to wrestle to take every thought captive, unto the obedience of Jesus Christ. We must discipline ourselves to recognize quickly traces of ungodly and unbiblical thinking. Much of our faith and thought activity goes on in our heart's "inner man," or "mission control center." Paul offers guidance throughout his writings of a God-honoring thought life, as in Phillipians 4:8:

> Finally, brothers, whatever is true, whatever is honorable, whatever is just, whatever is pure, whatever is lovely, whatever is commendable, if there is any excellence, if there is anything worthy of praise, think about these things.

Questions for Spiritual Formation:

1. Why could this chapter also be entitled, "The Spiritual Battle for Your Mind"?

2. Do you currently have any ideologies controlling your thought life? What from Scripture would attest that such ideologies are ungodly and false?

3. Why could the second part of the passage in this chapter ("take every thought captive to obey Christ"), also be considered, "Truth on the Guidance of the Mind"?

4. How can meditating on texts like Phillipians 4:8 genuinely begin to reform your thought habits? Paul writes, "Finally, brothers, whatever is true, whatever is honorable, whatever is just, whatever is pure, whatever is lovely, whatever is commendable, if there is any excellence, if there is anything worthy of praise, think about these things."

Shall Atheists Dare Insult the Cross?
By Isaac Watts

Shall atheists dare insult the cross
Of our Redeemer, God?
Shall infidels reproach His laws,
Or trample on His blood?

What if He choose mysterious ways
To cleanse us from our faults?
May not the works of sovereign grace
Transcend our feeble thoughts?

What if His Gospel bids us fight
With flesh, and self, and sin,
The prize is most divinely bright
That we are called to win.

What if the foolish and the poor
His glorious grace partake,
This but confirms His truth the more,
For so the prophets spake.

Do some that own His sacred Name
Indulge their souls in sin?
Jesus should never bear the blame,
His laws are pure and clean.

Then let our faith grow firm and strong,
Our lips profess His Word;
Nor blush nor fear to walk among
The men that love the Lord.[114]

---

[114]Isaac Watts, *Shall Atheists Dare Insult the Cross?*, (Public Domain, 1867).

Chapter 14

Knowledge of the Enemy

FORT HOOD, Texas – The insurgents gathered quietly just before dawn Nov. 4, in an isolated field, forming up into neat lines and placing their weapons at their feet. As the sun broke the horizon, they sank to their knees for morning prayers, asking for guidance and glory in their war against the American invaders. Another day of training on Fort Hood had begun.

This particular band of al-Qaida fighters had been wreaking havoc on an Army squadron all week – taking out multiple vehicles and entry control points with improvised explosive devices, killing dozens of U.S. soldiers in ambushes, and even capturing two vehicles. Their success came from a wealth of knowledge about their American adversaries – knowledge derived from the fact that they are also Army soldiers. For this week, however, they were playing the part of anti-American insurgents for Operation Bear Mountain, a week-long training exercise conducted by the 2nd Squadron, 38th Cavalry Regiment, 504th Battlefield Surveillance Brigade.

The unique training, tailored from enemy tactics, techniques, and procedures culled from a decade of war in Iraq and Afghanistan, requires the soldiers involved to immerse themselves in their roles as insurgents – which this group of soldiers did with relish. 'When [my soldiers] have to fight like the Taliban and think like the Taliban, they get motivated,' said 1st Sgt. Joseph Freccatore of Troop B. 'It's surprising.' Playing the role of insurgents provides valuable insight into the workings of the enemy, said Freccatore, noting that the liquidity of their operating procedures is one reason they can be effective against the much larger, better-equipped forces they're fighting.

Later that morning, the rag-tag bunch of mock terrorists planned a complex attack on the entry control point of a forward operating base a couple of miles from their mock training camp. The plan was to approach the gate as a group, feigning outrage over an unarmed civilian that's been shot and wounded by American troops. They wanted to escalate the noise and outrage of the protest and draw warning fire from the sentries, creating confusion. At this point Pfc. Michael Churach, who was rigged with a simulated explosive vest under his clothes, would approach the gate, offering information and hoping to get as close to a high-value target or group of soldiers as possible before 'detonating' (the mock vest made a loud beeping sound like a car alarm when a button was pushed).

The plan was rehearsed all morning. At 1 p.m. they walked up to the gate of the FOB yelling, waving sticks and throwing the occasional stone. The soldiers guarding the gate kept them back at first, but under the sustained commotion, Churach was eventually able to get close enough to rush the gate and push the button. Seven soldiers were 'killed.' Game over. Lesson learned.[115]

So, understanding and knowing their enemy helped one U.S. Army brigade to be better prepared to know the tactics of their enemy. Likewise, knowing what the apostle Paul says about the forces of spiritual darkness can help Christians to be best prepared to engage in the spiritual war that is raging around us each day.

Finally, be strong in the Lord and in the strength of his might. Put on the whole armor of God, that you may be able to stand against the schemes of the devil. *For we do not wrestle against flesh and blood, but against the rulers, against the authorities, against the cosmic powers over this present darkness, against the spiritual forces of evil in the heavenly places.* Therefore, take up the whole armor of God, that you may be able to withstand in the evil day, and having done all, to stand firm (Eph. 6:10-13, emphasis added).

From the apostle Paul's letter to the Christians at Ephesus, the sixth chapter of Ephesians contains the classic account of the spiritual armor of the saint that he or she must be aware of and understand the significance of. Christians are clothed with Jesus Christ and these items of the spiritual armor (6:13-20) likewise make up the life of faith and all that God has supplied our needs with. Looking into 6:12, the believer has added to his or her knowledge the *why* Paul calls for the church to stand and "take up" the battle armor to face the attacks from spiritual darkness in this world.

Verse 12 of chapter 6 is sandwiched between 11 and 13 where the author exhorts the Christians at Ephesus to "put on the whole armor of God" and to "take up the whole armor of God." Let

---

[115]Ken Scar, "Knowing Your Enemy: American Soldiers Train as Taliban," *Defense Visual Information Distribution Service,*
https://www.dvidshub.net/news/59758/knowing-your-enemy-american-soldiers-train-taliban.

this text be considered in two parts then: 1) negating the use of conventional warfare; and 2) recognizing the tactics of spiritual darkness.

Negating the Use of Conventional Warfare

Let's begin by looking at verse 12 that says our struggle is not against flesh and blood. One can quickly observe the clarification Paul is making here in his introduction to the section. I have titled this section "Negating the Use of Conventional Warfare" because here Paul is contrasting the idea that may not be clear to some, spiritual enemies require spiritual weapons to defeat them. Paul is stating something somewhat obvious, but there may be some readers that did not immediately recognize the method of conflict Paul was referring to. Under the tyranny of the Roman government, the Christians of Paul's day, both Jew and Gentile, would have been familiar with the mighty military conquests of Rome.

Paul states here, emphatically, our struggle is not against flesh and blood. If they were envisioning any type of literal, physical fighting or battling against representations of evil in the world, Paul was trying to make it clear for them. In saying "we do not wrestle against flesh and blood," and he is speaking of a type of fighting or wrestling that we engage in the daily battle of life. The word *wrestle* or *struggle* is the precise wording that describes the sport of wrestling or even combative wrestling (as in hand to hand combat).

In early Greek society and known to Paul was a wrestling event where the competitors were to ultimately secure victory over the opponent and pin him down with his hand upon his neck. This is an intensive physical conflict to beat the opponent and of course, here it refers to the struggle of the real Christian life. Against the world, the flesh, and the devil. Here the wrestling conflict we face is emphatically not a struggle in a normal flesh and blood physical competition against opposition (or more seriously, an enemy). It is more than that—it is against rulers, powers, and world forces of "this present darkness," and "spiritual forces of evil in the heavenly places." Calvin stated:

> The meaning is, that our difficulties are far greater than if we had to fight with men. There we resist human strength, sword is opposed to sword, man contends with man, force is met by force, and skill by skill; but here the case is widely different. All amounts to this, that our enemies are such as no human power can withstand. By flesh and blood the apostle denotes men, who are so denominated in order to contrast them with spiritual assailants. This is no bodily struggle.[116]

Now, there are certainly aspects of the wickedness and evil that oppose God that we face in flesh and blood. Perhaps we could describe some of these things as consequences, indicators, or even symptoms of the spiritual war that is raging against God and against all that is good and representative of God. One example of persecution, among many that could be named in recent years, comes from the Voice of the Martyrs' web site is the seven churches in Tanzania that were destroyed by fire in one area:

> Arsonists used gasoline as an accelerant to ensure that seven churches in northwestern Tanzania were destroyed in attacks on Sept. 22 and Sept. 27, 2015. Muslim extremists have repeatedly threatened Christians in the Bukoba district and want to "reduce" the number of churches in the area, says one pastor. Attackers set fire to three churches over two-hours on Sept. 22 in Kashfa village. Four mainline churches were also set alight just five days later on Sunday, Sept. 27. Two other churches burned on the same night were completely gutted. Pastor Vedasto Athanas of Living Water International

---

[116]Calvin, *Galatians and Ephesians*, 335-336.

Church stated that his 70-member church lost everything, including musical instruments and all of their chairs. The 35-member Evangelical Assemblies of God Tanzania church was also burned.

A VOM contact reported that this is the third arson attack that LWI church has suffered. Attacks on the church occurred earlier this year on April 4 and two years ago on Sept. 27, 2013. Both times, the church was ready to replace their tin structure with a concrete building, but the fires forced them to start over...

Church leaders say that one possible motive behind the arson attacks may be linked to tensions between Muslims and Christians in regards to animal slaughter. Muslim extremists in the region believe that it is forbidden for non-Muslims to slaughter animals, and have attempted to force Christians to buy their meat only from Muslims. Being forced to pay for meat-slaughtering is a burden on poor believers.

Another Christian leader suggests that local Muslim authorities are attempting to reduce the spread of Christianity and church growth. When churches have sought permission to build, they are often prevented by authorities who state that the areas have been zoned as 'residential areas.'[117]

So, as in those Tanzania church burnings, there are physical effects of spiritual war, or war raging against God. In wrapping up a first point of the chapter, we can see Paul's emphasis of there being not a physical flesh and blood struggle, which reminds us of our tendency to think in a humanistic way and less on the power of God in

---

[117]Voice of the Martyrs, "Tanzania, Arson Destroys 7 Churches," *Persecution News*, https://hisworldmissions.weebly.com/uploads/1/1/3/7/11371273/persecution_news_-_feb_2016.pdf.

the spiritual battle of life around us. Our human strength is nothing without God, yet men historically have raged of their perceived power.

Notice a few Holy Spirit inspired thoughts from the psalms that remind us of the weakness of all human strength: "His delight is not in the strength of the horse, nor his pleasure in the legs of a man, but the LORD takes pleasure in those who fear him, in those who hope in his steadfast love" (Psalm 147:10-11).

As well, regarding the deceptiveness of military strength alone: "Some trust in chariots and some in horses, but we trust in the name of the LORD our God" (Psalm 20:7). There is also the deception of trusting in political strength alone, apart from the Lord: "Put not your trust in princes, in a son of man, in whom there is no salvation. When his breath departs, he returns to the earth; on that very day his plans perish. Blessed is he whose help is the God of Jacob, whose hope is in the LORD his God, who made heaven and earth" (Psalm 20:7146:3-6). Last, it is a sham to put ones trust in some perceived strength in money, riches, or property (Psalm 52:6-7).

Recognizing the Tactics of Spiritual Darkness

In our introduction, we saw that soldiers benefitted militarily and tactically when they gained insights into how the Taliban fought and thought. They sharpened their skill by understanding the ways of the enemy. The apostle Paul sort of springboarded off of verse 11 of Ephesians 6, "Put on the whole armor of God," to stating his explanation or recognition of the tactics of the spiritual darkness in verse 12 "for we do not wrestle against flesh and blood."

The hinge on which the verse turns is the conjunction "but;" the contrast can be seen when looking at the verse again: "we do **not** wrestle against flesh and blood, **but** against the rulers, against the authorities…." Thus, the struggle the Christian man or woman faces is not this, but that…. This fight is about opposing all evil rulers, authorities, "cosmic powers over this present darkness," and "the spiritual forces of evil in the heavenly places."

189

Firstly, the struggle is not what it seems, humanistically speaking, but against "rulers" and what does that mean? The context tells us this is some type of world influence of evil. While Paul says here it is against the rulers, and authorities, and they are enemies of God. The "rulers"—your Bible may have the word, "principalities" (KJV)—speaks literally of a world monarch. This definitely has the sense of some evil authority in the world, including the spirit world. It could be related to the same order of evil angels; it is a governmental term (principality, ruler, and magistrate). However, the context of evil is outside of flesh and blood governing rule. Paul uses the term referring to angels and demons holding governmental dominions.

As well there is an understanding gained from Scripture regarding the demonic hosts that depicts a structure of the forces of hell, and that they are organized under a head figure. These passages include Revelation 12:7-9; Matthew 26:52-53; and Mark 5:7-10, 15-16.

> And crying out with a loud voice, he said, 'What have you to do with me, Jesus, Son of the Most High God? I adjure you by God, do not torment me.' For he was saying to him, 'Come out of the man, you unclean spirit!' And Jesus asked him, 'What is your name?' He replied, 'My name is Legion, for we are many.' And he begged him earnestly not to send them out of the country (Mark 5:7-10).

The definition of *legion* comes from a Roman military term of 6,000 infantry soldiers with additional calvary.

Another category of evil mentioned by Paul is "against powers," which is again, a type of rule or executive authority. Here there is an evil influence of wickedness. Paul uses the term also in Ephesians 1:21; Colossians 1:13. Here translated *domain*, as in "domain of darkness". The term is translated "authorities," referring to the Lordship of Jesus over all such authorities; they are subject to Jesus Christ. "For by him all things were created, in heaven and on earth, visible and invisible, whether thrones or dominions or rulers or *authorities*—all things were created through him and for him" (Col. 1:16, emphasis added).

As well, we war "against the cosmic powers over this present darkness" (Eph. 6:12) or "against the world forces of this darkness" (NASB). This is absolutely a satanic title if there ever was one, literally, a world leader of the darkness of the age. This additionally reminds the believer of the satanic hosts raging against the light of God. John uses a similar term here to describe the devil in John 14:30, calling Satan the "ruler of this world." This is a highly descriptive way to define the forces of evil.

Calvin said of this text 500 years ago, "The corruption of the world gives way to the kingdom of the devil, for he could not reside in a pure and upright creature of God, but arises from all sinfulness of men."[118] The darkness of the world here refers to the immorality or ungodliness of men. The last enemy of God mentioned by Paul is the phrase, "against spiritual forces of wickedness in the heavenly places" (Eph. 6:12, NASB). The ESV and NIV are very similar as well, "against the spiritual forces of evil [the spiritual things of wickedness] in the heavenly places/realms."

The attempts by the powers of evil to thwart the holy purposes of God are relentless. This last grouping is distinguished by them being in heavenly places (or realms). This is signifying the word for word *place*, respecting the very place of heaven or the celestial places above the sky and refer in this context to the place where demonic forces wage war against God Almighty. We may think of evil here fighting the Kingdom of God. In their book entitled *Spiritual Warfare*, Brian Borgman and Rob Ventura question:

> So what does Satan ultimately want to accomplish through his many schemes? He wants to destroy our faith in Christ...When Paul was anxious about the spiritual state of the new Thessalonian believers, he put it like this: "For this

---

[118]Calvin, *Galatians and Ephesians*, 335-336.

reason, when I could no longer endure it, I sent to know your faith, lest by some means the tempter had tempted you, and our labor might be in vain" (1 Thess. 3:5, emphasis added). Paul's fear was that Satan, the tempter, had so worked through the persecution the Thessalonians were experiencing that he had weakened their faith, thus making the apostle's labor among them fruitless. [119]

There is a stark reality to be deeply grasped of an actual spiritual war that is happening all around us (in our minds, marriages, families, churches, communities, in the workplace, throughout our nation, and the world). The battle that rages against the Lord Jesus Christ and His church requires us to be ever increasingly vigilant and alert. Consequentially, recall that the apostle Paul puts the guidance in the form of command verbs to "put on the whole armor of God" (Eph. 6:11), and to "take up the whole armor of God" (verse 13). These are calls to war—the enemy is certain. These are our orders from God. Christians will have victory over him as well if they battle against the enemy with the resources that Christ supplies (Eph. 6:10-13; Ja. 4:7; 1 Peter 5:9-10).

Pastor David Platt, pastor of McLean Bible Church in his "Secret Church Message" series on *Angels, Demons and Spiritual Warfare* affirms this reality of a spiritual war:

This is a cosmic spiritual war, which means that involvement in this spiritual war is inevitable...We sometimes think that spiritual warfare and demonic activity is something that happens when something weird starts to go on. Reality is spiritual warfare, [it] is happening when you are sitting alone at your computer or when you pick up the remote on your TV. When you wake up in the morning, and you turn to your spouse. When you look in your child's eyes. When you walk

---

[119]Brian Borgman and Rob Ventura, *Spiritual Warfare: A Biblical and Balanced Perspective*, (Grand Rapids: Reformation Heritage, 2014), 29.

to class, and you sit in your desk at work, spiritual warfare is happening. Not just at isolated weird times. The battle is continual. The battle is fierce, and spiritual retreat only leads to spiritual defeat. You cannot ignore this war, ladies and gentlemen. The Bible does not say ignore the devil, and he will flee from you.[120]

[120]David Platt, *Angels, Demons and Spiritual Warfare*, Secret Church, http://www.radical.net/resources-secret-church/secret-church-7-angels-demons-and-spiritual-warfare.

Questions for Spiritual Formation:

1. How would turning to the weapons of God, the armor of God, and the truth of God be considered figuratively to not be "conventional warfare"?

2. Why would the type of hostility and persecution that the VOM article reported be considered spiritual warfare? Why do some cultures with overt hostility to the gospel consider violent persecution as normal to the Christian life, while Western believers consider it very far from their Christian experience and their "right" to avoid?

3. Can you think of biblical reasons to be involved in recognizing the "tactics of spiritual darkness"?

4. How would the instruction by Jesus to love your enemies and to pray for them (Matt. 5:44) or the injunction by Paul to not be overcome by evil but overcome evil with good (Rom. 12:21) be considered spiritual warfare?

Gird on Thy Conquering Sword
by Philip Doddridge

Gird on Thy conquering sword,
Ascend Thy shining car,
And march, almighty Lord!
To wage Thy holy war.
Before His wheels in glad surprise,
Ye valleys rise, and sink, ye hills.

Fair truth, and smiling love,
And injured righteousness,
Under Thy banners move,
And seek from Thee redress;
Thou in their cause shalt prosperous ride,
And far and wide dispense Thy laws.

Before Thine aweful face
Millions of foes shall fall,
The captives of Thy grace—
The grace that captures all.
The world shall know, great King of Kings,
What wondrous things Thine arm can do.

Here to my willing soul
Bend Thy triumphant way;
Here every foe control,
And all Thy power display;
My heart, Thy throne, blest Jesus! see,
Bows low to Thee, to Thee alone.[121]

---

[121]Philip Doddridge, *Gird on Thy Conquering Sword*, (Public Domain, 1867).

Chapter 15

Spiritual Combat

In the Loving Labor of Parenting

Whether through political machinations such as those of Pharaoh and Herod, through military conquests in which bloodthirsty armies rip babies from pregnant mothers' wombs (Amos 1:13), or through the more "routine" seeming family disintegration and family chaos, children are always hurt. Human history is riddled with their corpses. Whether we look back over the pages of world history, or just around us today, the point bears true. Children are so often caught in the crossfire, so often hurt, so often the victims of a larger conflict in which they have no say, no influence, no responsibility. It happened back when primitive peoples thought slaying their children would appease the gods, and when war meant burning homes and sacking villages. And it happens still today when deranged citizens carry guns into elementary schools, and when abortion clinics welcome terrified teenagers with open arms, or when Boko Haram pillages another Nigerian village, or a young couple decides Down syndrome will disrupt their life plans...There is a war on children, and we are all, in one way or another, playing some role in it.[122]

---

[122]Jonathan Parnell, "Parenting Means wrestling Demons," *Desiring God Ministries*, http://www.desiringgod.org/articles/parenting-means-wrestling-demons.

I would absolutely agree that there is a war on children in this world, and much of western civilization has shown this sentiment through the sexual revolution, abortion, the widespread abolition of the sanctity of marriage, not to mention human depravity, sexual perversion, greed, and simple matters like the absence of agape love. Other cultural obstacles that children and their parents face include widespread feminized educational models in America, paranoia of the westernized and vastly boy related attention deficit disorder, or gender-neutral social engineering programming.

There has been much work done in studying boy and girl learning styles, and a shift to a more feminized form of education in our culture in recent generations that has led to much discussion and research. Christiana Hoff Summers in her significant book entitled *The War Against Boys* has provided much research and support for the notion that the shift to feminized education formats has led to a massive disadvantage and consequence in the education of boys in America. The book expresses that there is a crisis facing the education of boys in American culture. The author argues that in an effort to give greater societal advantages to girls, our culture has moved to a model that will have the effects of losing young men, through an attempt to punish boys through a feminized model that is not natural to innately male thinking and learning styles. The book argues:

> To address the problem, we must acknowledge the plain truth: boys and girls are different. Yet in many educational and government circles, it remains taboo to broach the topic of sex differences. Gender scholars and experts still insist that the sexes are the same and argue that any talk of difference only encourages sexism and stereotypes.[123]

---

[123]Christiana Hoff Summers, *The War Against Boys: How Misguided Feminism is Harming our Young Men*, (Simon & Schuster: New York, 2015), 1-2.

Psalm 127-A Song of Ascents. Of Solomon. Unless the LORD builds the house, those who build it labor in vain. Unless the LORD watches over the city, the watchman stays awake in vain. It is in vain that you rise up early and go late to rest, eating the bread of anxious toil; for he gives to his beloved sleep. Behold, children are a heritage from the LORD, the fruit of the womb a reward. *Like arrows in the hand of a warrior are the children of one's youth. Blessed is the man who fills his quiver with them! He shall not be put to shame when he speaks with his enemies in the gate* (emphasis added).

Though in no way do I desire to humiliate him, I want to include a personal story about my 16-year-old son. I recently reminded my wife—after our son threw a tantrum because he could not get to the beach fast enough for his desires—that we are in an intense spiritual battle for the minds and hearts of our children. Though many verses do not have a label above them saying, *this is a verse about parenting*, often just below the surface of the verse is a wonderful application that we can draw out for the work of shepherding our children. One verse that immediately came to mind was, "Be sober-minded; be watchful. Your adversary the devil prowls around like a roaring lion, seeking someone to devour" (1 Peter 5:8). I almost felt like the devil wanted to shake and bake my unsuspecting teenage son for lunch, and that I had much work to do in helping cultivate his personal walk with Jesus Christ.

If indeed, we are in an all-out spiritual war, and the devil is seeking someone to devour, why would the Christian parent not have an automatic protective desire to assume that the "father of lies" will be happy to take out our children one by one if we do not build a strategic spiritual defense plan? The needed fight for the family in the American home is at the crisis point. Let no Christian parents be naïve then that the "accuser of the brethren," who systematically de-

198

stroyed that righteous man Job (Job 1-2), will not fail to target any-one who desires to live a godly life in this present evil age. These hellish attacks of the wicked one, mingled with the ways of the fallen world and our depravity, are relentless.

Do not be deceived, if we are content to set aside the weapons of our warfare then we will most likely be caught unaware concern-ing the deceptions of the demonic. Again, from the cherished pas-sage on the armor of God, in the light of the great responsibility to raise God-fearing children in this age of opposition consider Ephe-sians 6:11. One could apply this to parenting where there is often a sense of spiritual warfare. The passage introduces that it is necessary to "put on the whole armor of God, that you may be able to stand against the *schemes* of the devil" (emphasis added).

In 2020, parents would be foolish and spiritually deaf/blind to ignore the reality of the demonic schemes that are described by Paul in 6:11. The definition of this phrase, "the schemes of the devil," is about these methods of the devil that the saint is to be aware of, alert to, and prepared to face in an outright attack. There are many verses that are specific in their scope towards parenting, such as Ephesians 6:1-2; Mark 9:42; Proverbs 13:24; 22:6; Deuteronomy 21:18-21, and more. However, there are many guidelines available in the untold number of texts and passages that apply directly to the Christian home and family life. There are many principles for the conduct and family values that the whole family is responsible to live out. Let's discuss ten of them.

10 Overarching Themes from the Bible for Christian Parenting

Agape self-sacrificial love is absolutely a primary code of conduct and an underlying parental need. This standard of selfless and unconditional love of a parent both emulates the character of Jesus and "covers a multitude of sin." This is the standard and life-long goal for every relationship. The apostle Paul writes:

Love is patient and kind; love does not envy or boast; it is not arrogant or rude. It does not insist on its own way; it is not irritable or resentful; it does not rejoice at wrongdoing, but rejoices with the truth. Love bears all things, believes all things, hopes all things, endures all things. Love never ends. As for prophecies, they will pass away; as for tongues, they will cease; as for knowledge, it will pass away (1 Cor. 13:4-8).

Pursuing personal holiness is an admonition found in Scripture that is for all believers to heed. *"You shall be holy, for I am holy"* (1 Peter 1:16) is the instruction. This pursuit in combatting worldliness, and personal defilements, is often debated and strong convictions have been held on varying views. There is a balance here to be sought away from legalism, and away from antinomianism (against law). The discerning parent will teach his or her child not necessarily what to think (a list of Do's and Don'ts), but rather to apply the Bible to their reasoning through principles of Scripture internalized. Another text that is often related to this aspiration to holiness is from Paul: "'All things are lawful,' but not all things are helpful. 'All things are lawful,' but not all things build up" (1 Cor. 10:23). In other words, not everything is spiritually profitable for us, though we may assert our freedoms to practice that thing (e.g., areas of music, movies, clothing, and friends).

Forgiveness is another action that must be both modeled by the parents and taught to the children to practice in their lives. It must be a way of life for parent-to-parent and parent-child relationships. It must be a marital and parental code. It is grievous to hear parents complain of a list of things they hold against their children. This is an indication of bitterness towards the child, unforgiveness, and a lack of agape love (which does not keep a list). The Bible has many passages that have the central theme of forgiveness. A few passages that demonstrate the urgency of forgiveness include the account of the brothers of Joseph pleading with him for forgiveness for their wickedness towards him (Gen. 50:17). As well, central to the Lord's

200

prayer and verses surrounding the cherished prayer: "And forgive us our debts, as we also have forgiven our debtors…. For if you forgive others their trespasses, your heavenly Father will also forgive you, but if you do not forgive others their trespasses, neither will your Father forgive your trespasses" (Matt. 6:12, 14-15). Additionally, consider Jesus's model of forgiveness from the cross (Luke 23:34), and the parable of the unforgiving servant:

Then Peter came up and said to him, "Lord, how often will my brother sin against me, and I forgive him? As many as seven times?" Jesus said to him, "I do not say to you seven times, but seventy-seven times. Therefore, the kingdom of heaven may be compared to a king who wished to settle accounts with his servants. When he began to settle, one was brought to him who owed him ten thousand talents. And since he could not pay, his master ordered him to be sold, with his wife and children and all that he had, and payment to be made. So the servant fell on his knees,   imploring him, 'Have patience with me, and I will pay you everything.' And out of pity for him, the master of that servant released him and forgave him the debt. But when that same servant went out, he found one of his fellow servants who owed him a hundred denarii, and seizing him, he began to choke him, saying, 'Pay what you owe.' So his fellow servant fell down and pleaded with him, 'Have patience with me, and I will pay you.' He refused and went and put him in prison until he should pay the debt. When his fellow servants saw what had taken place, they were greatly distressed, and they went and reported to their master all that had taken place. Then his master summoned him and said to him, 'You wicked servant! I forgave you all that debt because you pleaded with me. And should not you have had mercy on your fellow servant, as I had mercy on you?' And in anger his master delivered him to the jailers, until he should pay all his debt. So also my heavenly Father will do to every one of you, if you do not forgive your brother from your heart (Matt. 18:21-35).

201

Servant leadership is a model of true humility in leadership and a model found in Scripture in the life of Christ. Parental leadership comes with the inherent standard of serving the young lives that are growing up under the family's roof. Generally, parents do serve their children as a way of life, often sacrificing more for them. However, parents can often grow impatient with unreasonable expectations of their children. There is a danger of both being overly permissive and being overly authoritarian in parental leadership.

Parenting absolutely requires a tenderheartedness and graciousness in leading children that is described in the word *servant*. Servant leadership is a term that is fitting to describe how parents should lead. Parents need to be aware of when they are growing impatient and losing a humble perspective with their children as children are often very sensitive to hypocrisy. The Lord modeled servant leadership for the apostles:

Now before the Feast of the Passover, when Jesus knew that his hour had come to depart out of this world to the Father, having loved his own who were in the world, he loved them to the end. During supper, when the devil had already put it into the heart of Judas Iscariot, Simon's son, to betray him, Jesus, knowing that the Father had given all things into his hands, and that he had come from God and was going back to God, rose from supper. He laid aside his outer garments, and taking a towel, tied it around his waist. Then he poured water into a basin and began to wash the disciples' feet and to wipe them with the towel that was wrapped around him. He came to Simon Peter, who said to him, "Lord, do you wash my feet?" Jesus answered him, "What I am doing you do not understand now, but afterward you will understand." Peter said to him, "You shall never wash my feet." Jesus answered him, "If I do not wash you, you have no share with me." Simon Peter said to him, "Lord, not my feet only but also my hands and my head!" Jesus said to him, "The one who has bathed does not need to wash, except for his feet, but is completely clean. And you are clean, but not every one of you." For he knew who was to betray him; that was why he said, "Not all of you are clean." When he had washed their feet and put on his outer garments and resumed his place, he said to them, "Do you understand what I have done to you? You call me Teacher and Lord, and you are right, for so I am. If I then, your Lord and Teacher, have washed your feet, you also ought to wash one another's feet" (John 13:1-14).

As well, Jesus taught and modeled that this leadership must be rooted in humility: He taught that to be great was to be a servant, and ultimately a slave of all. The Lord modeled this in his redemptive and self-sacrificial passion to die for our sin. (Mark 10:43-45). There is no room in biblical parenting for arrogance, and when we ever are at fault or have sinned against our children, we must humble ourselves as a role model and ask their forgiveness for our sin. The reconciliation with one's children when sin has occurred is an imperative, and they must see the humble initiative of their parent in righting such wrongs.

Being a **Spiritual role model** in the study and learning of Scripture is imperative. Parents must teach and inspire their children by not only mandating their children to go to church to be taught and shepherded by pastoral leadership, but they must themselves provide pastoral leadership to their children. The father is absolutely to be a gentle and godly shepherd to his family. This is the very foundation of the church. The qualifications of an elder are vital, "He must manage his own household well, with all dignity keeping his children submissive, for if someone does not know how to manage his own household, how will he care for God's church?" (1 Tim. 3:4-5).

The home is the foundation for life and where children can learn a rich spiritual heritage that will prepare them for adulthood. From ancient Israel the Scriptures called for Hebrew parents to train their children in the Word of God:

And these words that I command you today shall be on your heart. You shall teach them diligently to your children, and shall talk of them when you sit in your house, and when you walk by the way, and when you lie down, and when you rise. You shall bind them as a sign on your hand, and they shall be as frontlets between your eyes. You shall write them on the doorposts of your house and on your gates. (Deut. 6:6-9).

Mentoring children in sexuality and gender roles is a requirement to intentionally help provide for your children in their childhood and youth. Young men need much supervision and to be taught what a Christian man should think and how to conduct himself. Similarly, girls and young ladies desperately need biblical femininity modeled for them. Both biblical masculinity and femininity in singleness and marriage are desperately needed today. Our world is going through an international crisis in the areas of sexuality and gender roles.

Not only is the world confused through years of revolt against the design and plan of God in the realms of maleness and femaleness, but also by rejection of the biblical models of motherhood and fatherhood, both still required to make babies, but also to raise them in the nurture and admonition of the Lord. (Eph. 6:4). From creation it is clear that God established a *"creation mandate,"* a simple foundation for civilization. Moses wrote under the inspiration of the Holy Spirit:

Then God said, "Let us make man in our image, after our likeness. And let them have dominion over the fish of the sea and over the birds of the heavens and over the livestock and over all the earth and over every creeping thing that creeps on the earth." So God created man in his own image, in the image of God he created him; male and female he created them. And God blessed them. And God said to them, "Be fruitful and multiply and fill the earth and subdue it, and have dominion over the fish of the sea and over the birds of the heavens and over every living thing that moves on the earth" (Gen. 1:26-28).

The counterculture ministry work of organizations like the Council of Biblical Manhood and Womanhood (https://cbmw.org/) have set a pace-setting example in American culture and throughout the world. The top four affirmations of their statement on their core beliefs about biblical sexuality and gender roles read:

A. Both Adam and Eve were created in God's image, equal before God as persons and distinct in their manhood and womanhood (Gen 1:26-27, 2:18).

B. Distinctions in masculine and feminine roles are ordained by God as part of the created order, and should find an echo in every human heart (Gen 2:18, 21-24; 1 Cor. 11:7-9; 1 Tim 2:12-14).

C. Adam's headship in marriage was established by God before the Fall, and was not a result of sin (Gen 2:16-18, 21-24, 3:1-13; 1 Cor.11:7-9).

D. The Fall introduced distortions into the relationships between men and women (Gen 3:1-7, 12, 16):

   i.   In the home, the husband's loving, humble headship tends to be replaced by domination or passivity; the wife's intelligent, willing submission tends to be replaced by usurpation or servility.

   ii. In the church, sin inclines men toward a worldly love of power or an abdication of spiritual responsibility, and inclines women to resist limitations on their roles or to neglect the use of their gifts in appropriate ministries."[124]

Parents would absolutely do well to teach their children this important aspect of the biblical model for the creation mandate by reinforcing the biblical differences in maleness and femaleness designed by the Creator.

Biblical financial management is an essential piece of the puzzle in what the parents aspiring to God-honoring parenting must desire to pursue as requirements for imparting wisdom to prepare their children with a biblical worldview for life that will endure the ways of the world and wiles of the devil. Personally, with 5 children, I feel this is a very difficult part, yet I know I must model for my kids a disciplined goal to spend carefully, tithe, give further to missions when possible, be aggressive about avoiding debt, have a good credit rating, invest wisely when possible, and other areas of family finances. Certainly, many ministries and individual authors have written on wise family finances. The Bible has many wise principles and standards for what financial principles are best for parents to teach to their children. Three biblical financial truths to start with and that are central to children having a personal theology of finances are:

1. *The love of money is a root of all kinds of evil* (1 Tim. 6:10). Teach your children to love God and worship Him alone. Teach them to "lay up their treasures in heaven." Teach them always to put God

---

[124]The Danvers Statement. http://cbmw.org/about/danvers-statement/, "The Danvers Statement summarizes the need for the Council on Biblical Manhood and Womanhood (CBMW) and serves as an overview of our core beliefs. This statement was prepared by several evangelical leaders at a CBMW meeting in Danvers, Massachusetts, in December of 1987. It was first published in final form by the CBMW in Wheaton, Illinois in November of 1988.

first in every part of their lives, and that money is a resource to manage and not to let it control their heart.

2. "The rich rules over the poor, and *the borrower is the slave of the lender*" (Prov. 22:7, emphasis added). Teach your children to keep their accounts short. To have the ability to completely pay for what they purchase and to be very careful with any credit-related situations, so that they do not enslave themselves in something that will have hurtful future ramifications. My children have heard my wife and me discuss bills and credit cards. Our older kids knew at times we had credit card debt, and that we worked making it a high priority to get out from under it. There is an absolutely freeing sense when all debt has been paid off, even when vehicle loans are totally paid in full. As a principle, there is a warning in Scripture about allowing yourself to be enslaved to debt. Prayerfully pursue wisdom about getting released from the bondage of debt, and celebrate when you are free from it.

3. Regularly *give your tithe or "first fruits" to God*. I will not go in depth about the tithe debate (whether 10% or more should absolutely be given to God in an offering). As a principle there is guidance in Scripture to take a portion right away and give it back to the Lord who blessed you with your income (or harvest). "Honor the LORD with your wealth and with the firstfruits of all your produce; then your barns will be filled with plenty, and your vats will be bursting with wine." (Prov. 3:9-10). Help them young to begin to honor the Lord with their finances.

The control of the mouth is a massive theme throughout the Bible. It is true: "A fool's mouth is his ruin" (Prov. 18:7). Teach your children to guard their mouths, to repent of foolish speech. Teach them there are words that tear down and destroy, but that we must be those who speak the words of life as, "Death and life are in the power of the tongue, and those who love it will eat its fruits" (18:21). The New Testament as well is replete with serious instruction for the management of our mouths. Those who tame the tongue will be known for their godliness:

> For we all stumble in many ways. And if anyone does not stumble in what he says, he is a perfect man, able also to bridle his whole body. If we put bits into the mouths of horses so that they obey us, we guide their whole bodies as well. Look at the ships also: though they are so large and are driven by strong winds, they are guided by a very small rudder wherever the will of the pilot directs. So also the tongue is a small member, yet it boasts of great things. How great a forest is set ablaze by such a small fire! And the tongue is a fire, a world of unrighteousness. The tongue is set among our members, staining the whole body, setting on fire the entire course of life, and set on fire by hell (James 3:2-6).

Brothers and sisters, pray for your children to learn to manage their mouths.

The stewardship of resources is of untold value. Certainly, this may go hand in hand with not being a lover of money, but this goes further into everything we are blessed with from our material possessions, things that belong to others, our time, our health, and more. If parents show their children how to take care of their belongings, they will see the value of our resources and as well be mindful to respect the things of others. If God has blessed me with it, it is worth taking care of.

Increase of this world's goods is from the Lord. "Yes, the LORD will give what is good, and our land will yield its increase" (Ps. 85:12). Yet, if it becomes an idol of our hearts, we have exchanged our walk with God for the worship of materialism. The Old Testament law contains many examples of guidance that may fall under "love for our neighbor." Consider the conscientiousness of being a steward of things belonging to or borrowed from your neighbor: "'If a man borrows anything of his neighbor, and it is injured or dies, the owner not being with it, he shall make full restitution'" (Ex. 22:14). This includes stewardship for your property and that of your neighbors, the law commands, "'You shall not move your neighbor's landmark, which the men of old have set, in the inheritance that you will hold in the land that the LORD your God is giving you to possess'" (Deut. 19:14).

Other factors such as our time, and the time that belongs to our children or others. I should be a wise steward of time in this sinful world, to discipline myself and teach my children to honor God with every day and every hour. "Look carefully then how you walk, not as unwise but as wise, making the best use of the time, because the days are evil" (Eph. 5:15-16).

Parental discipline is of the Lord. If a child is old enough to understand, he or she can discern the difference between corporate discipline, spanking, and child abuse. You have the opportunity to train them in thinking biblically. A child can understand at a young age that it is the will of God to receive correction, or discipline (including controlled spanking). Godly correction with discipline is a mark of parental love: "Whoever spares the rod hates his son, but he who loves him is diligent to discipline him" (Prov. 13:24).

The parent must teach the child to turn away from foolishness: "Folly is bound up in the heart of a child, but the rod of discipline drives it far from him" (Prov. 22:15). Proverbs is clear that corporate disciple applied by the parents to the child is the will of God:

"Do not withhold discipline from a child; if you strike him with a rod, he will not die" (23:13).

Questions for Spiritual Formation:

1. What may be some of the dynamics to the conflict between parenting and the "schemes of the devil"?

2. In what ways is biblical motherhood the perfect example of "servant leadership"? In what ways is biblical fatherhood truly "servant leadership"?

3. Why is the mentoring of our children in sexuality and gender roles especially important in westernized cultures today?

4. Considering James 3:6-10:

   And the tongue is a fire, a world of unrighteousness. The tongue is set among our members, staining the whole body, setting on fire the entire course of life, and set on fire by hell. For every kind of beast and bird, of reptile and sea creature, can be tamed and has been tamed by mankind, but no human being can tame the tongue. It is a restless evil, full of deadly poison. With it we bless our Lord and Father, and with it we curse people who are made in the likeness of God. From the same mouth come blessing and cursing. My brothers, these things ought not to be so.

   How is the "control of the mouth" specifically like a spiritual warfare act?

O God, my Refuge, Hear my Cries
by Isaac Watts

O God, my refuge, hear my cries,
Behold my flowing tears;
For earth and hell my hurt devise,
And triumph in my fears.

What inward pains my heart-strings wound,
I groan with ev'ry breath;
Horror and fear beset me round
Amongst the shades of death.

Let me to some wild desert go,
And find a peaceful home,
Where storms of malice never blow,
Temptations never come.

Vain hopes, and vain inventions all
To 'scape the rage of hell!
The mighty God on whom I call,
Can save me here as well.

By morning light I'll seek his face,
At noon repeat my cry,
The night shall hear me ask his grace,
Nor will he long deny.

God shall preserve my soul from fear,
Or shield me when afraid;
Ten thousand angels must appear
If he command their aid. [125]

---

[125]Isaac Watts, *O God, My Refuge, Hear my Cries*. (Public Domain, 1816).

211

Chapter 16

Wielding the Sword

The Progress of Growing in Grace

As the dark Middle Ages came to an end and the Renaissance loomed on the cultural horizon, the study of swordsmanship became a gentlemanly pursuit, rather than a military one, and Masters of Defense taught tactics that were more likely to be used in fights between two individuals rather than in a multi-person fight on the battlefield. In the 1400s, the demand for fighting schools expanded, and Milan, Venice, Verona, and Bologna all had schools taught by Masters of Defense. Under the Masters' tutelage, combat methodologies became more sophisticated and streamlined, due in part to technological advances in combat weaponry and armament, as well as the proliferation of firearms, and an increasingly armed and educated middle class.

Using new materials and construction, swordsmiths produced weapons lighter than their Medieval predecessors, and the thus the rapier became the primary sword type to be used by the Masters of Defense. Because of its light weight and exceedingly thin body, the rapier moved sword fighting from large, broad strokes to the finer, more accurate thrusting approach…The advances in combat technology led to a decrease in military training for broadsword and other spear or bladed weapons. Instead, swordsmanship became the pursuit of gentlemen interested in learning the scientific art of sword fighting…English Master George Silver wrote in 1599, "A

Master of Defense is he who can take to the field and know that he shall not come to any harm."[126]

As established in Chapter 2 on "The Sword of the Spirit: The Word of God," there is a precision and seasoned skill in applying the truth and wisdom of Scripture to the daily routine of life, to relationships, and to the wrestling with sin. Scripture asserts the Bible as the very Word of God and a sword (i.e., "the sword of the Spirit"). As Hebrews 4:12 emphasizes, "For the word of God is living and active, sharper than any two-edged sword, piercing to the division of soul and of spirit, of joints and of marrow, and discerning the thoughts and intentions of the heart."

Therefore, the skilled practitioner of the swordsmanship of Scripture to life, the seasoned pilgrim and gospel warrior, must progress and become quite consistent and proficient in the wielding of the sword of the Spirit. The cycle on the following pages is a practical outworking of a general pattern of the nature of temptations and trials in life. It is not exhaustive in any form, but rather demonstrates the manner of the battle with the temptation of sin in the heart, and the frustrating and trying nature of various trials and tribulations in life. It demonstrates the challenge of self-confrontation for the Christian man or woman that would desire to grow in grace.

---

[126]L.A. Jennings, "The Italian Renaissance of Swordsmanship, Wrestling, and Boxing," *Fightland.* http://fightland.vice.com/blog/the-italian-renaissance-of-swordsmanship-wrestling-and-boxing.

The Cyclical Nature of the Confrontation of Sin and Trial
*Experiencing Temptations and Tests

Do you know your provocations?
1. Be ready to respond biblically (James 1:12-15).
2. Trust in God (1 Cor. 10:13).
3. Recognize the temptation/potential damage (Prov. 4:23).
4. Beware of self-deception/rationalization of sin (Gen. 3:1-4).

**The consolation and challenge
for the true believer**
1. Obtain excellent wisdom (Prov.1:20-33).
2. Continuously follow the Lord (Phil. 3:12-14).
3. Aspire to holiness (Rom. 12:1-2; 6:12-18).
4. Recognize being forgiven (Rom. 8:1).

Use your spiritual reflexes
1. Fortify a mindset for spiritual war (2 Cor. 10:5).
2. Face sin/temptation w/ courage; be aggressive (Gen.39:6-10).
3. Know the urgency to guard against sin (Gen. 4:6-8).

The self-confrontation in sin and test
1. Take responsibility (Col. 3:9-10).
2. Be honest (1 John 1:8, 10; 3:6-9).
3. Confess sin promptly (1 John 1:8-10).

Meditations to help deal with sin: (1 Peter 1:13-15; Matt. 15:18, 20; James 1:2-4; Mark 7:20-23; Heb. 12:14-17; 1 Cor. 6:11)

Explanation of the Cyclical Nature
of the Confrontation of Sin and Trials

Temptations and tests are inevitable in the life of the believer. We will find such tests and will fight against sin in life. Job says "But man is born to trouble as the sparks fly upwards" (Job 5:7). The great problem and the spiritual responsibility that human beings bear is the perpetual nature of facing such problems. Truly, the temptation toward sin is different from the difficulty of the manifold trials of life. It was recognized in the above cycle that sin and the temptation to sin do not have God for their source. In other words, sin has not begun in the mind of God; this should not confuse. The Bible says in 1 Corinthians 14:33 that, "God is not a God of confusion but of peace." It can be recognized that God "himself does not tempt anybody" (James 1:13-15).

Looking at the "trials" or tests that God allows and causes: such tests exist in our life for various reasons. About such tests, consider verses like James 1:2-4 to be instructional; here is learned "the test of your faith." As well, consider Romans 8:28. In the design of the heart of God is His plan for each situation in the life of the believer.

One other example is Genesis 50:20. It is remembered that in the life of Joseph, his brothers did wickedness toward him, and sold him as a slave, but God guided him to Egypt and exalted Joseph in a positional way in Egyptian society to a place of tremendous influence for the protection and future of Israel. This recognizes the cyclical nature of facing forms of trials, which subsequently are situations in life initiated or caused in some form by the providential hand of God. Nevertheless, there are enough situations of temptation to sin caused by our "flesh"—or of the dark nature of the world, or by the devil himself in his worldly manifestations—of which we will face regularly.

Next, in studying the points of the cycle described, consider the first area of such a cyclical pattern as being when (in time) we experience the temptations and tests in life. The question proposed for contemplation is: Do you know your provocations? This is a fundamental understanding of self.

1) ***Be ready to respond to such situations biblically*** If one is saturated in the Word of the Lord, he or she will be prepared in mind to face a temptation. Again, consider James 1:12-15 that says we are tempted of our same passions and wicked desires, but blessed is the man who perseveres under the test. James also reminds us that God has a prepared gracious arrangement to reward those who endure spiritually.

2) A second element in this portion of the cycle is ***trusting God***. One must trust God in the test or temptation to sin because the Scriptures say that He is going to guide us by means of the test (1 Cor. 10:13). He will provide a "route of escape" in the situation.

3) A third element is ***to recognize a temptation and potential damage*** it can cause in one's life and the lives of others (Prov. 4:23). We need to know our own inclinations to sin or to fail in such manner of tests. Watching over our hearts in this way will keep us aware of the propensity towards sin and its destructive manner.

4) Lastly, remember ***to beware of self-deception and the rationalization of sin.*** We need to recognize our same potential to lie to ourselves like Adam and Eve in the garden (Gen. 3:1-4). Adam and Eve fell to self-deception, it led to their blaming others for their sin (Eve blamed the devil and Adam blamed the woman and God). In this one may recognize his or her own provocations.

Use your spiritual reflexes to *respond* to the temptation biblically. This is an important step in the cycle. Here, one recognizes that there is a temptation to sin or that one is in the midst of a trial.

1) *Fortify a mentality for spiritual war* and do so immediately. One way we do that is by taking every thought captive to obey Christ (2 Cor. 10:5). There is a spiritual war every day in the life of the believer in his or her relationships, mind, place of work, and community. One needs to destroy false teachings, ungodly thoughts, and unbiblical philosophies. The spiritual battle is an ideological battle.

2) *Face sin or temptation with courage and aggressiveness* is the second element necessary in using spiritual reflexes to combat sin or temptation. It is recorded that Joseph needed to reject the temptation immediately and to judge the situation instinctively with the perception of sanctity. He did not want to sin against God or his supervisor (Gen. 39:6-10).

3) Third, *know the urgency to guard against sin.* In the relationship between Cain and Abel, there was conflict. Cain had jealous anger against his brother. He recognized that the Lord looked with acceptance toward Abel and his offering. Cain stewed in his anger, his countenance had fallen, and his sin consumed him to the point of killing Abel (Gen. 4:6-8). The urgency to guard against sin is to respond *before* the sin destroys the life of the person.

The self-confrontation in sin and test is the next step. Let's look more closely at each of the three elements and examine ourselves.

1) *Take responsibility* for any sin or temptation. Confess. Repent. Believers have the responsibility to reject the old man and to put on

217

the clothing of the new man (Col. 3:9-10). The biblical responsibility of ownership of sin or of the inclinations or actions of sin is part of this *self-confrontation* that the Bible admonishes believers to (James 1:13-15).

2) **Be honest** with yourself, with others, and most importantly, with God. He already knows anyway. Always remember that God hates lies (Prov. 14:5; Acts 5:1-11;1 John 1:8, 10; 3:6-9). The believer is exhorted to judge himself as to whether he is improving in sin-opposing qualities (2 Peter 1:10-11).

3) **Confess sin promptly** to the Lord. Due to the fall (Gen. 3:1-8), all have a sinful nature, and need to confess sin immediately to God (1 John 1:8-10). Also, in the case of the test, if pertinent, should include the confession of the preoccupation or fear about the test (Phil. 4:6-7).

The consolation and challenge for the true believer is the fourth section and concludes the chart of the cyclical nature of facing temptation and the tests of life. The consolation and challenge are the work of persevering through the substance of the temptation or trials. (James 1:2-4).

1) **Obtain excellent wisdom** in order to grow in the spiritual life (Prov. 1:20-33; Prov. 8:10-11). The experience of trials and temptations is the opportunity to increase in wisdom and maturation in Christ via the catalyst of the adversity (Malachi 3:2-3; 1 Peter 1:7).

2) **Continuously follow the Lord** so we grow spiritually. We overcome the temptation or trial in a victorious manner when we continue in Christ with a faithful heart (Phil. 3:12-14). We need to follow the Lord and not lose heart and grow in an eternal perspective, and thus ultimately become overcomers. (2 Cor. 4:16-17; Rev. 3:12, 21).

3) Third, *aspire to holiness* in order to never serve sin. Aspire toward the victorious route of overcoming in Christ to expel fear, worry, or anxiety in a spiritual test. In aspiring to holiness, one is surrendering oneself to the conformity to the will of God (Rom. 12:1-2; 6:12-18).

4) *Recognize being forgiven* completely in Christ is the final element in this section of the cycle. Though our sinfulness is not eradicated from our nature, God has wiped away our sin (Rom. 8:1). Believers are already not guilty because Christ has paid for their sin.

In conclusion, consider that in our responsibility to pursue Christ, and the way of holiness, God will maintain faithfulness in His working in us, to perfect us, until Christ comes (Phil. 1:6).

---

[127]Monsieur L'Abbat, *The Project Gutenberg Ebook of the Art of Fencing*, 2004. (Public domain).

Questions for Spiritual Formation:

1. In this consideration of the cyclical nature of sin and trials in the Christian life, why would it be vital to know your own provocations or triggers?

2. How are the actions of "fortifying a mentality for spiritual war," "facing sin or temptation aggressively," and "knowing the appropriate sense of urgency about the situation to guard against sin" like developing and using your "spiritual reflexes"?

3. Why would taking personal responsibility over the issue, crisis, or temptation be a step of self-confrontation in the testing of your faith or tempting you face (Col. 3:9-10)?

4. Why is the last part of the cycle listed probably the most important—the consolation and challenge for the true believer "persevering by means of the temptation or trials"? (i.e., continuing to follow the Lord, pursuing holiness and wisdom, understanding forgiveness)?

Press Forward, O Soldiers
by Fanny J. Crosby

Press forward, O soldiers, with banner and shield;
The Lord is our helper the world is our field;
With courage advancing, our strength in His might,
Let this be our watchword: "For God and the right."

Move forward, O soldiers, be loyal and true,
Whatever the trials keep Jesus in view;
His steps let us follow, and walk in His light,
And this be our watchward: "For God and the right."

Though legions of darkness may rally their pow'rs,
Though fierce be the conflict, the day shall be ours;
God's arm is our refuge; we'll trust in His might,
While marching to battle for "God and the right."

Chorus:

Then stand for the right,
Firmly stand for the right;
And this be our watchword:
"For God and the right."[128]

---

[128]Fanny Crosby, *Press Forward, O' Soldiers* (Public Domain, 1899).

Chapter 17

The Goal of Our Work

The End of Spiritual Warfare

In military training, many often receive injuries on and off the battlefield. Of course, some have been greatly injured, limbs amputated and suffered more extensive injuries. The path to recovery, healing, and restoration of function can be very difficult for some, and for others, it can become a way of life. On the web site for the University of South Dakota's doctoral program on physical therapy, the site explains the goals of physical therapy. It states, "Physical Therapy is concerned with the prevention of disability and the restoration of function following disease, injury, or loss of function. The goal of physical therapy is to help patients reach their maximum performance potentials while learning to live within the limits of their capabilities. Physical therapy, the science of healing and art of caring, involves evaluation, treatment planning, performance of tests and measures, client education, consultative services, and supervision of support personnel." [129] You may have been injured and gone through a season of physical therapy or know someone who has. There is a goal for a person to avert a disability or handicap. After someone has had a serious illness, trauma, or has lost a physical ability, the purpose of physical therapy is *to restore* that ability or function. Restoration is a primary goal of physical therapy. This chapter sets forth the goal of the ministerial labor of love. This goal is seen

---

[129]University of South Dakota, *Physical Therapy*, http://catalog.usd.edu/preview_entity.php?catoid=20&ent_oid=1054#Physical_Therapy.

in the spiritual responsibilities of evangelism, apologetics, and discipleship.

Him we proclaim, warning everyone and teaching everyone with all wisdom, that we may present everyone mature in Christ. For this I toil, struggling with all his energy that he powerfully works within me (Col. 1:28-29).

In the epistle to the Colossian Church (written from AD 60-62), the apostle Paul, it is strongly held, communicated the words through writing while imprisoned for the Christian faith in Rome. In the first chapter of this beloved "prison epistle," Paul explains that by the very same gospel of hope that the Colossians have heard, he was called by God to be an apostle and minister of Jesus Christ. He continues in verses 25-27 that to him was entrusted the privilege of making known the mysteries of Christ. As well, it is this very same Jesus, the oft-quoted phrase, "Christ in you, the hope of glory" that Paul writes of in verse 27. He says in verse 28, "Him we proclaim" (ESV), or "we proclaim Him" (NASB). This very same Jesus is the One Paul is proclaiming to the Colossian Church and all believers down through the ages.

Before diving into three specific parts of Colossians 1:28-29—on the warning, teaching, and struggling for the purposes of Jesus—let it be considered how Paul begins this verse, "Him we proclaim." The KJV reads, "Whom we preach," perhaps best capturing the sense. Both have identical implications, pointing back to Jesus. It is the primary subject of the preaching of Paul, and the subject of every pastor, preacher, chaplain, evangelist, and missionary down through the corridors of time who labored—and continue to labor—to carry the message of Christ crucified.

This preaching that Paul refers to is a literal "announcing, declaring, a making known," to those listening. The same wording is used in Acts 13:5 when it was described how Paul and Barnabas were sent as missionaries by the early church in Antioch. "So, being sent out by the Holy Spirit, they went down to Seleucia, and from there they sailed to Cyprus. When they arrived at Salamis, they proclaimed the word of God in the synagogues of the Jews. And they had John to assist them" (Acts 13:4-5). They arrived and began to tell, announce, declare, and make known the saving message of the cross of Jesus Christ.

Paul here in Colossians is merely summarizing their ministry focus to ultimately lead every believer to a place of spiritual maturity in Christ. We will look at the emphasis of this further on in the chapter, but first to consider the three activities that Paul uses to describe the life of gospel ministry work (warning, teaching, and struggling).

On Warning All the People

Onto the first business of warning. Paul expresses, "Him we proclaim, *warning* everyone" (Col. 1:28, emphasis added). One may ask the questions, "What is this warning that the apostle is talking about?" and "Do we have details here that can help us to determine in what way?" Paul is writing that they were warning everyone (literally, every man, all, anyone). This warning in the context here describes a wonderful thrust that Paul particularly uses repeatedly; it is a well-traveled path, a common term used by the apostle. The verse indicates that Paul and his missionary companions were warning everyone and speaks of exhortation or admonishment. It means to put something into one's thinking, "to caution them or reprove them gently." Here Paul says the minister of the gospel is exhorting everyone towards the idea of repentance, to consider their morality. This is one part of what Paul said their announcing Jesus to people was involved with.

Another example is when Paul reminds the believers at Ephesus (as he was saying goodbye to them in Acts 20:31) how he had warned them and admonished them for 3 years. This describes a continuous warning, exhorting and encouraging (*noutheteo*) them about matters of the gospel and here specifically of pleading with them not to be swayed by false teachers that would come in to deceive and destroy. Luke, the author of Acts, writes:

I know that after my departure fierce wolves will come in among you, not sparing the flock; and from among your own selves will arise men speaking twisted things, to draw away the disciples after them. Therefore, be alert, remembering that for three years I did not cease night or day *to admonish* every one with tears (Acts 20:29-31, emphasis added).

Again, Paul uses the same idea of warning in 1 Corinthians 4:14. Paul appeals to the Corinthian believers that he is an apostle and their servant and he loves them as a spiritual father. In challenging them in their faith, he is warning them, admonishing them in the Lord. The apostle was exhorting them in a fatherly way to emulate his example in the faith.

Lastly in Colossians 3:16, this wording is used another time by Paul in teaching the Colossian Christians to engage in a certain way of life. He wrote, "Let the word of Christ dwell in you richly," calling for the Christian community to live out this behavior of the Word of God-inspired living. He challenged them to be about teaching one another and admonishing (exhorting, encouraging) one another "in all wisdom, singing psalms and hymns and spiritual songs, with thankfulness in your hearts to God" (Col. 3:16).

This warning/admonishing note is used repeatedly through the book of Proverbs as an overarching theme. In fact, chapters 1-9 have a general tone of this fatherly admonishment. As a principle, we read it in verses like 3:1; 4:1; 7:1. Here is one such example of this parental admonishment tone:

Then they will call upon me, but I will not answer; they will seek me diligently but will not find me. Because they hated knowledge and did not choose the fear of the LORD, would have none of my counsel and despised all my reproof, therefore they shall eat the fruit of their way, and have their fill of their own devices. For the simple are killed by their turning away, and the complacency of fools destroys them; but who-ever listens to me will dwell secure and will be at ease, with-out dread of disaster (Prov. 1:28-33).

On Teaching All the People

The apostle goes on, "Him we proclaim, warning everyone and *teaching everyone* with all wisdom" (Col. 1:28, emphasis added). This teaching that Paul is talking about is not complicated, it means *plainly, to instruct others as a teacher* ("to impart instruction," "to instill doctrine," "to explain," "to expound"). Notice here that *teaching* is described as "in all wisdom." One can sense clearly how, in light of this, we can grow in the Christian life. We are to be teachable, able to receive the teachings of God. Remember again, this teaching is all in the context of how Paul began the verse: "Him, we proclaim."

On this theme of the essentiality of teaching men the Bible, the Presbyterian Bible teacher Barnes commented:

> Paul made it his business to instruct men, as well as to exhort them. Exhortation and warning are of little use where there is not sound instruction and a careful inculcation of the truth. It is one of the duties of the ministry to instruct men in those truths of which they were before ignorant; see Mat. 28:19; 2Ti. 2:25.[130]

Scripture calls for believers to be taught, discipled, and trained up in the way they should go. From childhood, children in the church are formed in the loving teaching of Scripture, many coming to a genuine faith and continuing their learning on into adulthood. Others coming to faith in adolescence or adulthood would continue to grow and increase in spiritual learning.

---

[130]Barnes, *Albert Barnes Notes*, (Col 1:28).

In this context of the preaching of Christ crucified, this warning, this teaching, is going on (and again with the goal being all men coming to maturity in Christ). One example comes from Acts 15:35: "But Paul and Barnabas remained in Antioch, teaching and preaching the word of the Lord, with many others also." Additionally, Acts 18:9-11 explains: "And the Lord said to Paul one night in a vision, 'Do not be afraid, but go on speaking and do not be silent, for I am with you, and no one will attack you to harm you, for I have many in this city who are my people.' And he stayed a year and six months, *teaching the word of God* among them." (Acts 18:9-11, emphasis added). Both these texts illustrate the point—Paul was a diligent Bible teacher.

On Struggling with a Divine Purpose

The rest of the focal passage, Colossians 1:29, reads, " For this I toil, *struggling with all his energy that he powerfully works within me*" (emphasis added). In this remainder of the text, along with this warning and teaching, Paul says he is in toil and struggling for the cause of Christ. Here is a word mentioned earlier in chapter 11 of 1 Timothy 6:12: "Fight the good fight of the faith." Colossians 1:29 contains the same word, here translated "struggle" (ESV) or "striving" (KJV) in the portion, "For this I toil, *struggling* with all his energy." Again, the term, αγωνιζομενος, he is "struggling" to do this thing. Once more, this is a favorite word of Paul's; he says, "I am struggling, I am agonizing, all to see Christ formed in the hearts of others."

This struggling is a powerful athletically related word, meaning, literally "to contend in athletic games," "to agonize," "to struggle" or "to strive." Another usage of the term is found in Paul's letter to the Colossians 4:12: "Epaphras, who is one of you, a servant of Christ Jesus, greets you, always struggling on your behalf in his prayers, that you may stand mature and fully assured in all the will of God." Here he uses this term to describe the arduous prayer life of Epaphras to the saints in Colossae. Epaphras labored over them, striving for them in prayer before the throne room of God. The NASB says he is "always laboring earnestly" on their behalf in his prayer life. Remember also, the larger issue at hand in the text is that all believers may come to completeness and maturity in Christ.

Paul demonstrates this is the purpose of Christ in the reconciliation of salvation in the relationship between God and man. This is seen in Colossians 1:21-22: "And you, who once were alienated and hostile in mind, doing evil deeds, he has now reconciled in his body of flesh by his death, in order to present you holy and blameless and above reproach before him." One can see here the heart of a spiritual father, he is greatly concerned for the spiritual protection and the healthy development of the Christians he is providing leadership to. That is the model for every Christian leader today, to desire to warn, teach, and struggle on behalf of other Christians until they come to the place of maturity in the Lord.

Again, the goal—just as the example that I used from the description of the work of physical therapy being to lead others to the maximum potential of their physical capabilities—here in 1:28 is that we may present every man complete in Christ. This is the holy work of warning, teaching, and struggling to see people led to spiritual maturity. This was the goal of Paul and is the goal of every Christian leader, whether they consider themselves (or are considered by the church) to be "full-time" ministers of the gospel in some form or not. The goal, again, is seeing others led to maturity in Christ. That was the goal of Paul and the other apostles and it must be our goal, all to the glory of God.

The English churchman, Charles Simeon, commented on this text, and this goal:

> He sought to present them also perfect through his grace. This was the end at which our blessed Lord aimed in dying for sinners and the very same was the Apostle's end in preaching to them. He would not have his converts to continue in a low state of holiness, but to attain the fullest conformity to the Divine image: he would have them to "be holy,

even as He which had called them was holy 1Pe. 1:15-16." This is the more usual acceptation of the term "perfect" in the sacred volume: it means that growth which Christians in general may be expected to attain: it imports maturity, in opposition to infantine weakness. And so anxious was the Apostle to bring his converts to this state, that he continued "travailing, as it were, in birth with them," till it was fully accomplished.[131]

As well, it must be understood that every Christian soul is responsible for accomplishing this work. Some are babes and children in Christ and are just beginning to walk in the ways of the Lord, some are "young men" and feel passionately the challenge to stand and defend the Word of God in a dark world, and a lesser number are "fathers" in the faith, laboring maturely in a greater measure of knowledge of the Lord and walk with Him (1 John 2:12-14). All are somewhere on the journey, either growing in this process or facilitating the spiritual growth process of others.

In closing, just as clarification, spiritual maturity is not sinless perfection (as some have mistakenly thought). In Colossians 1:28, Paul states that the goal is to present every man complete in Christ. That wording, *complete*, means "mature," like a man of full age. This refers to being "spiritual adults in Christ" and no longer babies as the author of Hebrews states:

About this we have much to say, and it is hard to explain, since you have become dull of hearing. For though by this time you ought to be teachers, you need someone to teach you again the basic principles of the oracles of God. You need milk, not solid food, for everyone who lives on milk is unskilled in the word of righteousness, since he is a child. But solid food is for the mature, for those who have their

---

[131]Charles Simeon, *Horae Homiletica*, (Public Domain, 1832).

powers of discernment trained by constant practice to distinguish good from evil. Therefore, let us leave the elementary doctrine of Christ and go on to maturity, not laying again a foundation of repentance from dead works and of faith toward God (Heb. 5:11-6:1).

Questions for Spiritual Formation:

1. How is part of the goal of physical therapy "the restoration of function following disease, injury, or loss of function" like that of the spiritual goal of leading Christians to full maturity in Christ?

2. How is exhortation or admonishment of the believer desired to see led to maturity important? In what ways are we to be warned?

3. How is teaching the Scriptures a critical element to see other formed in their faith and walk with Christ?

4. What is the struggling and striving that Paul talked of in this process of helping others to grow in Christ unto maturity?

More Holiness Give Me
by Phillip Bliss

More holiness give me,
More sweetness within,
More patience in suff'ring,
More sorrow for sin,
More faith in my Savior,
More sense of His care,
More joy in His service,
More freedom in prayer.

Chorus:
Come, my Savior, and help me,
Comfort, strengthen and keep me;
Thou each moment wilt save me,
Thou art saving me now.

More gratitude give me,
More trust in the Lord,
More zeal for His glory,
More hope in His Word,
More tears for His sorrows,
More pain at His grief,
More meekness in trial,
More praise for relief.

Chapter 18

Epilogue: Final Thoughts on
Biblical vs. Errant Views
on Spiritual Warfare

As has been the emphasis of this book, and since we "wrestle not with flesh and blood," the focus of the believer in the spiritual war of the Christian life is upon the truth of the holy gospel of Jesus Christ crucified for sinners. The focus is always to be upon God, and not a preoccupation with chasing demons and attacking Satan in any way. Scripture clearly advocates that the course of action of the saint is always and ever, "Submit yourselves therefore to God. Resist the devil, and he will flee from you" (James 4:7). The focus of Scripture when it comes to this war—to include the normal development of growing in holiness and spiritual maturity—is upon the Word and drawing near to God.

No evil thing can exist in the holy presence of our sovereign and omnipotent God and Creator. The psalmist wrote of the place of the presence of God: "You make known to me the path of life; in your presence there is fullness of joy; at your right hand are pleasures forevermore" (Ps. 16:11). You will recall that David spoke much of running to the fortress of the Almighty. That was his recourse; he did not talk about fighting with demons and binding Satan. From Psalm 18:2, David, the warrior-king prayed and sang: "The LORD is my rock and my fortress and my deliverer, my God, my rock, in whom I take refuge, my shield, and the horn of my salvation, my stronghold."

The reader should sense that this book definitely has the feel of both applied Christian apologetics, and of spiritual warfare simultaneously. That is because our Defender in the fight is God Almighty, and our weapons are the truth of the Bible and prayer. Consider in these final remarks, the text on the spiritual armor. All of the protection of this spirit warrior is tied to a believer's relationship with God and the truth that is of God, from his or her "helmet of salvation" to the "sword of the Spirit, which is the Word of God" (Eph. 6:13-18). In a sense, the Christian life should resound as a *Victory March* in light of the victory won at the cross, yet believers live in the tension of the completed victory on Calvary and life in the fallen world bearing a corrupted and renewed *Imago Dei*.

The general area of spiritual warfare in the Bible is mostly seen as comprehensively focused on the reading, hearing, studying, meditating, and memorizing the Word of God. The Word that is "sharper than a two-edged sword" (Heb. 4:12) contains the message of redemption, the wisdom of God, and the history of the saga of the covenant-keeping God. The counterfeit work of the Holy Spirit found in the prosperity gospel teachers' attempts to brings other forms of spiritual warfare often through commanding God, binding Satan, slaying in the spirit, and casting out demons through direct confrontation with the demonic hosts.

Notice the vast focus upon you fighting and personally defeating demonic assailants. As well other, and purportedly mainstream, charismatic leaders have brought a distorted perspective of the Christian life through their perception of spiritual warfare. One article entitled "Demonology in the Pentecostal Charismatic Movements"[132] described much of spiritual warfare perspectives in the Charismatic movement. The article addresses the teaching of C. Peter Wagner who in his book, *Engaging the Enemy: How to Fight and Defeat Territorial Spirits* ...makes the claim, 'The growing interest

---

[132]Dan Boyce, *Demonology in the Pentecostal Charismatic Movements*, https://www.scribd.com/doc/30553142/Demonology-in-the-Pentecostal-Charismatic-Movements.

among scholars, pastors, missionaries, evangelists, and lay Christians in strategic-level spiritual warfare cries out for research and teaching' ...Wagner writes, "the subject of territorial spirits and world missions is surfacing on the agendas of many church, seminary and mission leaders."[133] The article goes on in the discussion of the believer engaging much in the aggressive work of binding territorial spirits. It is observable here, the example that there is much found in missiological practices of attacking Satan and demons, which is not seen in the Bible. The article states:

...the emphasis is on the need to become knowledgeable about how the demonic realm affects the individual. Their concern is for the believer to become free of the defiling work of demons in the believer's life...deliverance is no longer a sign of power much akin to divine healing. Rather it is to become a way of life for those who take seriously the call to holiness. This is especially evident in the Hammond's [writing] when one examines their chart, "Common Demon Groupings". The chart lists fifty-three main headings with two to twenty sub-listings in each group. Some of the "common demon groupings" are, bitterness, strife, jealousy, passivity, mind-binding, hyper-activity, sexual impurity, and religious.[134]

Again, the point being that nowhere in Scripture is there instruction from God that calls for people to bind spirits, fight demons personally, and focus their thoughts on attacking Satan. As well, though in an unprecedented way, the Lord Jesus Christ (and to some degree the apostles) personally talked to and confronted demons. The entire remaining body of the New Testament does not prescribe, command, or instruct Christians to engage in personally attacking or fighting Satan or demons.

Once more we are called to the truth of Scripture as our resistance, the mighty defense of God as our refuge, and the work of

---

[133]Boyce, "Demonology," 8.
[134]Ibid, 8-9.

prayer. In the excellent book by David Powlison entitled *Power Encounters: Reclaiming Spiritual Warfare*, he explains that "there is no direct command to do EMM (Ekballistic mode of ministry), even to relieve suffering." Powlison articulates that the New Testament confrontation with demons was not regarding the believer overcoming personal issues with sin. Therefore, the charismatic trend to fight demons and cast out demons (for example, the demon of anxiety, greed, or mental illness) is not on target with Scripture. He explains, "Scripture loudly rejects applying Ekballistic methods to include our warfare with sin…EMM advocates, in contrast, have radically redefined the purposes of demon deliverance-redefining human nature, God, and the devil along the way- without biblical warrant." [135]

As well, this includes the charismatic trend to approach healing in the same way, through some type of ekballistic healing that could involve binding demons of sickness, slaying in the spirit, or commanding God to heal. Again, Powlison does not advocate in his book that Ekballistic activity like demonic exorcism is presumed in Scriptture to be an ongoing ministry practice. To the contrary, the clear and abundant instruction is remembering to fervently pray, worship, study the Scriptures, and apply all of the guidance of the Bible to our decisions, emotional, psychological, materialistic and relational problems, sins, and needs.

In the classic work by C.S. Lewis, *The Screwtape Letters*, a senior demon is mentoring a junior demon to progress the accomplishments of their demonic agenda. Literarily brilliant, in their mentor/mentoree relationship is found great insights into the ways of evil, sin, and human depravity. In one portion on the wonders of God's love and the satanic opposition to divine love, "the Enemy's idea of love…," in sarcasm, the senior demon ponders:

---

[135]David Powlison, *Power Encounters: Reclaiming Spiritual Warfare* (Grand Rapids: Baker Books, 1995). 28-38. "Eckballistic comes from the Greek word *ekballo*, which means to "cast out". From *ek*- out- we get "exit." And from *ballo*, which means to throw or cast- we get "*ballistic.*" A ballistic missile is "thrown" into tits trajectory and then falls in an arc as gravity pulls it."

the Enemy's idea of Love is a contradiction in terms, what becomes of my reiterated warning that He really loves the human vermin and really desires their freedom and continued existence?... The truth is I slipped by mere carelessness into saying that the Enemy really loves the humans. That, of course, is an impossibility. He is one being, they are distinct from Him. Their good cannot be His. All His talk about Love must be a disguise for something else—He must have some real motive for creating them and taking so much trouble about them. The reason one comes to talk as if He really had this impossible Love is our utter failure to out that real motive...And there lies the great task. We know that He cannot really love: nobody can: it doesn't make sense. If we could only find out what He is really up to. [136]

---

[136]C.S. Lewis, *The Screwtape Letters*, (New York: The Macmillan Company, 1962), 87-88.

Facing A Task Unfinished
by Frank Houghton

Facing A Task Unfinished
That Drives Us To Our Knees
A Need That, Undiminished
Rebukes Our Slothful Ease
We, Who Rejoice To Know Thee
Renew Before Thy Throne
The Solemn Pledge We Owe Thee
To Go And Make Thee Known

We Bear The Torch That Flaming
Fell From The Hands Of Those
Who Gave Their Lives Proclaiming
That Jesus Died And Rose
Ours Is The Same Commission
The Same Glad Message Ours
Fired By The Same Ambition
To Thee We Yield Our Powers

Oh Father Who Sustained Them
Oh Spirit Who Inspired
Saviour, Whose Love Constrained Them
To Toil With Zeal Untired
From Cowardice Defend Us
From Lethargy Awake!
Forth On Thine Errands Send Us
To Labour For Thy Sake.[137]

---

[137]Frank Houghton, *Facing the Task Unfinished* (Public Domain, 1930).

Appendix A

Gleanings from *The Christian Soldier*
by Puritan Thomas Watson[138]

The Christian Soldier; or Heaven Taken by Storm (Part 3, by Reading and Hearing the Word)

1. We must provoke ourselves to *reading of the word*. What an infinite mercy it is that God hath honoured us with the Scriptures! The barbarous Indians have not the oracles of God made known to them; they have the golden mines, but not the Scriptures which are more to be desired 'than much fine gold,' Psalm xix. 10. Our Savior bids us 'search the Scriptures', John v.39. We must not read these holy lines carelessly, as if they did not concern us, or run over them hastily, as Israel ate the passover in haste; but peruse them with reverence and seriousness. The noble Bereans did 'search the Scriptures daily,' Acts xvii.11. The Scripture is the pandect of divine knowledge; it is the rule and touchstone of truth; out of this well we draw the water of life. To provoke to a diligent reading of the word, labor to have a right notion of Scripture.

Read the word as a book made by God Himself. It is given 'by divine inspiration' 2 Tim. iii.16. It is the library of the Holy Ghost. The prophets and apostles were but God's amanuenses or notaries to write the law at his mouth. The word is of divine original, and reveals the deep things of God to us. There is a numen, or sense of deity engraven in man's heart and is to be read in the book of the creatures; *quaelibet herba Deum*; but who this God is, and the Trinity of persons in the Godhead, is infinitely, above the light of reason; only God Himself could make this known. So for the incarnation of

---

[138]Thomas Watson, *The Christian Soldier*, (public domain, 1816), https://www.fivesolas.com/Watson/soldier4.htm.

Christ; God and man hypostatically united in one person; the mystery of imputed righteousness; the doctrine of faith: what angel in heaven, who but God himself, could reveal these things to us? How this may provoke to diligence and seriousness in reading the word which is divinely inspired. Other books may be written by holy men, but this book is indicted by the Holy Ghost.

Read the word as a perfect rule of faith; it contains all things essential to salvation. "I adore the fullness of Scripture," saith Tertullian. The word teaches us how to please God; how to order our conversation in the world. It instructs us in all things that belong either to prudence or piety. How we should read the word with care and reverence, when it contains a perfect model and platform of religion and is "able to make us wise unto salvation" (2 Tim. 3:15)!

When you read the word, look on it as a soul-enriching treasury. Search here as for a 'vien of silver' Prov. ii.4. In this word are scattered many divine aphorisms; gather them up as so many jewels. This blessed book helps to enrich you; it fills your head with knowledge, and your heart with grace; it stores you with promises: a man may be rich in bonds. In this field the pearl of price is hid: What are all the world's riches compared to these? Islands of spices, coasts of pearl, rocks of diamonds? These are but the riches that reprobates may have, but the word gives us those riches which angels have.

Read the word as a book of evidences. -- How carefully doth one read over his evidences! Would you know whether God is your God? search the records of Scripture, 1 John iii. 24. 'Hereby we know that he abides in us.' Would you know whether you are heirs of the promise? you must find it in these sacred writings. 2 Thes. Ii. 13. 'He hath chosen us to salvation through sanctification.' They who are vessels of grace, shall be vessels of glory.

Look upon the word as a spiritual magazine, out of which you fetch all your weapons to fight against sin and satan. 1. Here are weapons to fight against sin. The word of God is a consecrated sword that cuts asunder the lusts of the heart. When pride begins to lift up itself, the sword of the Spirit destroys this sin, 1 Peter iv. 5 'God resists the proud.' When passion vents itself, the word of God, like Hercules's club, beats down this angry fury: Eccles. V. 9. 'Anger rests in the bosom of fools.' When lust boils, the word of God cools that intemperate heat, Ephes. V. 5. 'No unclean person hath any inheritance in the Kingdom of Christ.' 2. Here are weapons to fight against Satan. The word fenceth off temptation. When the devil tempted Christ, he three times wounded the old serpent with the sword of the Spirit. 'Tis written, Matt. Iv. 7. Satan never sooner foils a Christian than when he is unarmed, and without Scripture weapons.

Look upon the word as a spiritual glass to dress yourselves by: It is a looking-glass for the blind, Psalm xix. 8. In other glasses you may see your faces; in this glass you may see your hearts, Psalm cxix. 104. 'Through Thy precepts I get understanding. This looking-glass of the word clearly represents Christ; it sets him forth in his person, nature, offices, as most precious and eligible, Cant.vi. 16. 'He is *altogether lovely*; he is a wonder of beauty, a paradise of delight. Christ who was veiled over in types, is clearly revealed in the mirror of the Scriptures.

Look upon the word as a book of spiritual receipts. Basil compares the word to an apothecary's shop, which has all kinds of medicines and antidotes. If you find yourselves dead in duty, here is a receipt, Psalm cxix. 50. 'Thy word hath quickened me.' If you find your hearts hard, the word doth liquify and melt them; therefore it is compared to fire for its mollifying power, Jer. xxiii. 29. If you are poisoned with sin, here is an herb to expel it.

Look upon the word as a sovereign elixer to comfort you in distress. It comforts you against all your sins, temptations, and afflictions. What are the promises but divine cordials to revive fainting souls. A gracious heart goes feeding on a promise as Samson on the honey-comb, Judges xiv. 9. The word comforts against sickness and death, 1 Cor xv. 55. 'O death, where is thy sting?' A Christian dies embracing the promise, as Simeon did Christ, Heb. xi. 13.

Read the word as the last Will and Testament of Christ. Here are many legacies given to them that love him; pardon of sin, adoption, consolation. This Wwill is in force, being sealed in Christ's blood. With what seriousness doth a child read over the will and testament of his father, that he may see what is left him.

Read it as a book by which you must be judged: John xii. 48. 'The word that I have spoken shall judge him at the last day.' They who live according to the rules of this book, shall be acquittéd; they who live contrary to them, shall be condemned. There are two books God will go by, the book of Conscience, and the book of Scripture: the one shall be the witness, and the other the judge. How should every Christian then provoke himself to read this book of God with care and devotion! This is that book which God will judge by at the last. -- They who fly from the word as a guide, shall be forced to submit to it as a judge.

2. The second duty of religion wherein we must provoke ourselves, is, in *hearing of the word.* We may bring our bodies to the word with ease, but not our hearts without offering violence to ourselves. When we come to the word preached, we come to a business of the highest importance, therefore should stir up ourselves and hear with the greatest devotion. Constantine the emperor was noted for his reverent attention to the word: Luke xix. 48. 'All the people were very attentive to hear him.' In the Greek it is 'they hung upon his lip.'-- When the word is dispensed, we are to lift up the everlasting doors of our hearts that the King of glory may enter in.

1. How far are they from offering violence to themselves in hearing, who scarce mind what is said, as if they were not at all concerned in

the business: they come to church more for custom than conscience: Ezekiel xxxiii. 31. 'They come to thee as the people cometh, and they sit before thee as my people, and they hear thy words, but they will not do them.' If we could tell them of a rich purchase, or of some place of preferment, they would diligently attend; but when the word of life is preached, they disregard it.

2. How far are they from offering violence to themselves in hearing, who come to the word in a dull, drowsy manner, as if they came to church to take a receipt to make them sleep. The word is to feed; it is strange to sleep at meat. The word judgeth men: it is strange for a prisoner to fall asleep at the bar. To such sleepy hearers God may say, *sleep on*. He may suffer them to be so stupefied, that no ordinance shall them: Matt. iii. 25. 'While men slept, his enemy came and sowed tares.' The Devil is never asleep, but sows the tares of sin in a drowsy hearer.

That we may, when we come to the word, offer violence to ourselves, and stir up ourselves to hear with devotion, consider,

1. It is God that speaksto us. If a judge gives a charge upon the bench, all listen.-- If a king speaks, all pay attention. When we come to the word, we should think thus with ourselves, we are to hear God in this preacher. Therefore Christ is said, now to speak to us from Heaven, Heb. xii. 25. -- Christ speaks in his ministers, as a king speaketh in the person of his ambassador. When Samuel knew it was the Lord that spake to him, he lent an ear, 2. Sam. iii. 5. 'Speak Lord, thy servant heareth.' They who slight God speaking in His word shall hear him speaking in his wrath, Psalm ii. 5. 'Then shall he speak unto them in his wrath.'

2. Let us consider the weightiness of the mattersdelivered to us. As Moses said to Israel, Deut. xxx. 19. 'I call Heaven and Earth to record this day, that I have set before you life and death.' We preach to men of Christ and of eternal recompenses; here are the *magnalia*

legis, the *weighty matters of the law*; and doth not all this call for serious attention? There is a great deal of difference between a letter of news read to us, and a letter of special business, wherein our whole land and estate is concerned. In the word preached our salvation is concerned; here we are instructed to the kingdom of God, and if ever we will be serious, it should be now: Deut. xxxvii. 47. 'It is not a vain thing for you, because it is your life.'

3. If the word be not regarded, it will not be remembered. Many complain they cannot remember; here is the reason, God punisheth their carelessness in hearing with forgetfulness. He suffers Satan to take away the word from them, Matt. xiii. 4. 'The fowls of the air came and devoured the seed.' The Devil is no recursant; he comes to church, but it is not with any good intent; he takes away the word from men. How many have been robbed of the sermon and their souls both at once.

4. It may be the last time that God will ever speak to us in His word; it may be the last sermon that ever we shall hear; and we may go from the place of hearing, to the place of judging. Did people think thus when they come into the house of God; perhaps this will be the last time that God will counsel us about our souls, the last time that ever we shall see our minister's face, with what devotion would they come! how would their affections be all on fire in hearing? We give great attention to the last speeches of friends. A parent's dying words are received as oracles. Oh let all this provoke us to diligence in hearing; let us think this may be the last time that *Aaron's bell* shall sound in our ears and before another day, we shall be in another world.

The Christian Soldier, (Part 4, by Prayer and Meditation)

3. The third duty wherein we are to offer violence to ourselves, is in prayer. Prayer is a duty which keeps the trade of religion flowing. When we either join in prayer with others, or pray alone, we must use holy violence; not eloquence in prayer, but violence carries it. Theodorus, speaking of Luther, 'once (says he) I overheard him in prayer: but, (good God), with what life and spirit did he pray! It was with so much reverence, as if he were speaking to God, yet with so much confidence, as if he had been speaking to his friend.' There must be a stirring up of the heart,

1.To prayer. 2. In prayer.

1. A stirring up of the heart to prayer, Job xi. 13. 'If thou prepare thine heart, and stretch out thine hands toward him.' This preparing of our heart by holy thoughts and ejaculations. The musician first tunes his instrument before he plays.

2. There must be a stirring up of the heart in prayer. Prayer is a lifting up of the mind and soul to God, which cannot be done aright without offering violence to one-self. The names given to prayer imply violence. It is called *wrestling,* Gen. xxxii. 24. and a *pouring out of the soul,* 1 Sam. i. 15. both of which imply vehemency. The affection is required as well as invention -- The apostle speaks of an effectual fervent prayer, which is a parallel phrase to *offering violence.*

Alas, how far from offering violence to themselves in prayer, 1. That give God a *dead, heartless* prayer. God would not have the blind offered, Mal. i. 8; as good offer the blind is as offering the dead. Some are half asleep when they pray, and will a sleepy prayer ever awaken God? Such as mind not their own prayers, how do they think that God should mind them? Those prayers God likes best which come seething hot from the heart.

2. How far are they from offering violence, who give God *distracted* prayer? while they are praying, they are thinking of their shop and trade. How can he shoot right whose eye is quite off the mark? Ezek. xxxiii. 31. 'Their heart goeth after their covetousness.' Many are casting up their accounts in prayer, as Hieram once complained of himself. How can God be pleased with this? Will a king tolerate that, while his subject is delivering a petition, and speaking to him, he should be playing with a feather? When we send our hearts on an errand to Heaven, how often do they loiter and play by the way? This is a matter of blushing. That we may offer violence to ourselves and by fervency feather the wing of prayer, let these things be duly weighed.

1. The majesty of God with whom we have to do. He sees how it is with us in prayer, whether we are deeply affected with those things we pray for. 'The king came in to see the guests,' Matt. xxii.11. So when we go to pray, the King of glory comes in to see in what frame we are; he has a window which looks into our breasts, and if He sees a dead heart, he may turn a deaf ear. Nothing will sooner make God's anger wax hot than a cold prayer.

2. Prayer without fervency and violence is no prayer; it is *speaking,* not *praying*. -- Lifeless prayer is no more prayer than the picture of a man is a man. To say a prayer, is not to pray; Ashanius taught his parrot the Lord's Prayer. Ambrose saith well, 'It is the life and affection in a duty that baptizeth it, and gives it a name.' 'Tis the violence and wrestling of the affections that make it a prayer, else it is no prayer. But a man may say as Pharaoh, 'I have dreamed a dream,' Gen. xli.15.

3. The zeal and violence of the affections in prayer best suits God's nature. He is a *spirit,* John iv. 24. and sure that prayer which is full of life and spirit is the *savory meat he loves*, 1 Peter ii. 5. 'Spiritual sacrifices acceptable to God.' Spirituality and fervency in duty, is like the spirits of wine, which are the more refined part of the

245

wine. *Bodily exercise profits nothing.* 'Tis not the stretching of the lungs, but the vehemency of the desire, that makes music in God's ears.

4. Consider the need we have of those things which we ask in prayer. We come to ask the favor of God; and if we have not his love, all that we enjoy is cursed to us. We pray that our souls may be washed in Christ's blood, and if he wash us not, 'we have no part in him.' Such are these mercies that if God deny us, we are forever undone. Therefire what violence therefore we need to put forth in prayer? When will a man be earnest, if not when he is begging for his life?

Let it provoke violence in prayer, to consider, that those things which we ask, God hath a mind to grant. If a son ask nothing but what his father is willing to bestow, he may be the more earnest in his suit. We go to God for pardon of sin, and no work is more pleasing to him than to seal pardons. Mercy is *his delight*, Micah vii. 18. We pray to God for a holy heart, and this prayer is according to his will, 1 Thes. iv. 3. 'This is the will of God, even your sanctification'. We pray that God would give us a heart to love him. How pleasing must this request needs be to God! This, if any thing, may excite prayer, and carry it in a *fiery chariot* up to Heaven, when we know we pray for nothing but that which God is more willing to grant than we are to ask.

6. No mercy can be bestowed on us but in a way of prayer. Mercy is purchased by Christ's blood, but it is conveyed by prayer. All the promises are bonds made over to us, but prayer puts these bonds in suit. The Lord has told Israel with what rich mercy He would bespangle them; he would bring them to their native country and that with *new hearts,* Ezek. xxxvi. Yet this tree of the promise would not drop its fruit, till shaken with the hand of prayer, verse 67. For 'all this yet be inquired.' The breast of God's mercy is full, but prayer must draw the breast. Surely, if all other ways are blocked up, there's

no good to be done without prayer; how then should we ply this oar, and by a holy violence stir up ourselves to take hold of God.

7. 'Tis only violence and intenseness of spirit in prayer that has the promise of mercy affixed to it, Matt vii. 7. 'Knock, and it shall be opened.' Knocking is a violent motion. The Aediles among the Romans had their doors always standing open, so that all who had petitions might have free access to them. God's heart is ever open to fervent prayer. Let us then be fired with zeal, and with Christ pray *yet more earnestly*. 'Tis violence in prayer that makes Heaven-gates fly open, and fetcheth in whatever mercies we stand in need of.

8. Large returns God has given to violent prayer. The dove sent to Heaven has often brought an olive leaf in its mouth: Psalm xxxiv. 6. 'This poor man cried, and the Lord heard him.'. Crying prayer prevails. Daniel in the den prayed and prevailed. Prayer did shut the lion's mouth and opened the lion's den. Fervent prayer (saith one) has a kind of omnipotency in it. Sozomen said of Apollonius, that he never asked anything of God in all his life that he did not obtain. Sleidan reports of Luther, that perceiving the interest of religion to be low, he betook himself to prayer; at length rising off his knees, he came out of his closet triumphantly, saying to his friends, *Vicimus, Vicimus, We have overcome; we have overcome*. At which time it was observed that there came out a proclamation from Charles the Fifth, that none should be further molested for the profession of the gospel. How may this encourage us and make us hoist up the sails of prayer when others of the saints have had such good returns from the holy land.

That we may put forth this holy violence in prayer, it is requisite there be a renewed principle of grace. If the person be graceless, no wonder the prayer is heartless. -- The body while it is dead hath no heat in it: while a man is dead in sin, he can have no heat in duty.

247

2. That we may be the more violent in prayer, it is good to pray with a sense of our wants. A beggar that is pinched with want, will be earnest in craving alms. -- Christian, review thy wants; thou wantest an humble, spiritual frame of heart; thou wantest the light of God's countenance; the sense of want will quicken prayer. That man can never pray fervently who does not pray feelingly. How earnest was Samson for water when he was ready to die, Judges xv. 18. 'I die for thirst.'

3. If we would be violent in prayer, let us beg for a violent wind. The Spirit of God is resembled to a *mighty rushing wind,* Acts ii. 2. Then we are violent, when this blessed wind fills our sails, Jude, verse 20. -- *Praying in the Holy Ghost.* If any fire be in our sacrifice, it comes down from heaven.

The fourth duty wherein we must offer violence to ourselves is *meditation*; a duty wherein the very heart and life-blood of religion lies. St. Bernard calls meditation *animae viaticum,* a bait by the way. Meditation may be thus described; it is an holy exercise of the mind; whereby we bring the truths of God to remembrance, and do seriously ponder upon them and apply them to ourselves. In meditation there are two things:

1. A Christian's retiring of himself, a locking himself, up from the world. Meditation is a work which cannot be done in a crowd.

2. It is a serious thinking upon God. It is not a few transient thoughts that are quickly gone, but a fixing and staying of the mind upon heavenly objects: this cannot be done without exciting all the powers of our souls, and offering violence to ourselves.

We are the more to provoke ourselves to this duty, because:

1. Meditation is so cross to flesh and blood. Naturally we shun holy meditation. To meditate on worldly, secular things, even if it were

248

all day, we can do without any diversion: but to have our thoughts fixed on God, how hard do we find it? How do our hearts quarrel with this duty? What pleas and excuses we have to put it off? The natural averseness from this duty shows that we are to offer violence to ourselves in it.

2. Satan does what he can to hinder this duty. He is an enemy of meditation. The devil cares not how much we hear, nor how little we meditate. Hearing begets knowledge, but meditation begets devotion. Meditation doth ballast the heart and makes it serious, while Satan labors to keep the heart from being serious. What need therefore is there of offering violence to ourselves in this duty? But methinks I hear some say, when they sit alone they do not know what to meditate about. I shall therefore furnish them with matter for meditation.

1. Meditate seriously upon the corruption of your nature. We have lost that pure quintessential frame of soul that we once had. There is a sea of sin in us. Our nature is the source and seminary of all evil: like Peter's sheet, wherein were 'wild beasts and creeping things,' Acts x. 12. This sin cleaves to us as a leprosy. This original pollution makes us guilty before the Lord; and even though we would never commit actual sin, it merits hell. The meditation of this would be a means to pull down our pride. -- Nay, even those who have grace have cause to walk humbly because they have more corruption in them than grace: their dark side is broader than their light.

2. Meditate seriously upon the death and passion of Christ. His soul was overcast with a cloud of sorrow when he was conflicting with his Father's wrath; and all this we should have suffered, Isaih liii. 5. 'He was wounded for our transgressions.' As David said, 'Lo, I have sinned, but these sheep, what have they done?' 2 Sam. xxiv. 17. So we have sinned, but this Lamb of God - what had he done?

1. The serious meditation of this would produce repentance. How could we look upon him 'whom we have pierced,' and not mourn over him? When we consider how dearly our sins cost Christ; how should we shed the blood of our sins which shed Christ's blood?

2. The meditation of Christ's death would fire our hearts with love to Christ. What friend shall we love, if not him who died for us? His love to us made him to be cruel unto himself. As Rebecca said to Jacob, Gen. xxvii. 13. 'Upon me, be thy curse.' So said Christ, 'upon me, be thy curse,' that poor sinners may inherit the blessing.

3. Meditate on your evidences for Heaven. What have you to shew for Heaven, if you should die this night? 1. Was your heart ever thoroughly convinced of sin? Did you ever see yourself lost without Christ? *Conviction is the first step to conversion,* John vii. 16. 2. Hath God ever made you willing to take Christ upon his own terms? Zech vi. 13. 'He shall be a priest upon his throne.' Are you as willing that Christ should be upon the throne of your heart to rule as well as a priest at the altar to intercede? Are you willing to renounce those sins to which the bias of your heart doth naturally incline? Can you set those sins, as Uriah, in the forefront of the battle to be slain? Are you willing to take Christ *for better and for worse?* to take him with his cross, and to avouch Christ in the worst of times? 3. Do you have the indwelling presence of the Spirit? If you have, what hath God's Spirit done in you? Hath it made you of another spirit? meek, merciful, humble? Is it a transforming Spirit? Hath it left the impress of its holiness upon you? These are good evidences for Heaven. By these, as by a spiritual touchstone, you may know whether you have grace or no. Beware of false evidences. None are further from having the true pearl, than they who content themselves with the counterfeit.

4. Meditate upon the uncertainty of all sublunary comforts. Creature-delights have their flux and reflux. How oft doth the sun of worldly pomp and grandeur goes down at noon. Xerxes was forced to fly away in a small vessel, who but a little before wanted sea-room for

his navy. We say everything is mutable; but who meditates upon it? The world is resembled to 'a sea of glass mingled with fire' Rev. xv. 2. Glass is slippery; it has no sure footing; and glass mingled with fire is subject to consume. -- All creatures are fluid and uncertain, and cannot be made to fix. What is become of the glory of Athens, the pomp of Troy? 1 John ii.17. 'The world passeth away:' It slides away as a ship in full sail. How quickly doeth the scene alter? and a low ebb succeed a high tide? There's no trusting to anything. Health may turn to sickness; friends may die; riches may take wings. We are ever upon the tropics. -- The serious meditation of this, would, 1. Keep us from being so deceived by the world. We are ready to set up our rest here, Psalm xliv. 11. 'Their inward thought is, that their houses shall continue for ever!' We are apt to think that our *mountain stands strong*. We dream of an *earthly eternity*. Alas, if we would meditate on how casual and uncertain these things are, we should not be so often deluded. Have not we seen great disappointments; and where we have thought to suck honey, there have we not drunk wormwood.

2. The meditation of the uncertainty of all things under the sun, would much moderate our affections to them. Why should we so eagerly pursue an uncertainty? Many take care to get a great estate; it is uncertain whether they shall keep it. The fire may break in where the thief cannot: or if they do keep it, it is a question whether they shall have the comfort of it. They lay up for a child; that child may die; or if he live, he may prove a burden. This seriously meditated on, would cure the dropsy of covetousness; and make us sit loose to that which hangs so loose and is ready to drop from us.

3. The meditation of this uncertainty would make us look after a certainty: that is, the getting of grace. This holy 'anointing abides,' 1 John ii. 27. Grace is a flower of eternity…Death does not destroy grace but transplant it and makes it grow in better soil. He that has true holiness can no more lose it than the angels can, who are fixed stars in glory.

5. Meditate on God's severity against sin. Every arrow in God's quiver is shot against it. Sin burned Sodom and drowned the old world. Sin kindles hell. If when a spark of God's wrath flies into a mans conscience, it is so terrible, what is it when God 'stirs up all his wrath'? Psalm lxxviii. 38. The meditation of this would frighten us out of our sins. There cannot be so much sweetness in sin, as there is sting. How dreadful is God's anger! Psalm xc. 11. 'Who knoweth the power of his wrath'? All fire, compared with the fire of God's wrath. is painted and imaginary. O that every time we meddle with sin, we would think to ourselves we choose the bramble, and fire will come out of this bramble to devour us.

6. Meditate on eternal life, '1 John ii. 25. This is his promise, even eternal life.' Life is sweet, and this word *eternal* makes it sweeter. This lies in the immediate vision and fruition of God. 1. This is a *spiritual* life: it is opposite to that animal life which we live now. Here we hunger and thirst; but there we 'shall hunger no more' Rev. vii. 16). There is the marriage supper of the Lamb, which will not only satisfy hunger, but prevent it. That blessed life to come does not consist in sensual delights, meat, and drink, and music; nor in the comfort of relations; but the soul will be wholly swallowed up in God, and acquiesce in him with infinite complacency. As when the sun appears, the stars vanish, so when God shall appear in his glory and fill the soul, then all earthly sensitive delights shall vanish. 2. It is a *glorious* life. The bodies of the saints shall be enameled with glory: they shall be made like Christ's glorious body, Phil. iii. 21. And if the cabinet be of such curious needle-work, how rich shall the jewel be that is put into it! how bespangled with glory shall the soul be! Every saint shall wear his white robe, and have his throne to sit upon. Then God will put some of his own glory upon the saints. Glory shall not only be revealed *to* them, but in them, Rom. viii.18). And this life of glory shall be crowned with eternity; what angel can express it! O let us often meditate on this.

1. Meditation on eternal life would make us labor for a spiritual life. The child must be born before it is crowned. We must be *born of the Spirit;* before we are crowned with glory.

2. The meditation on eternal life would comfort us in regard to the shortness of natural life. Our life we live now, flies away as a shadow: it is called a *flower*, Psalm ciii. 15. a *vapour*, James iv. 14. Job sets forth fragile life very elegantly in three of the elements, *land, water, and air*, Job ix. 25,26. Go to the land, and there man's life is like a swift post. Go to the water, there man's life is like a ship under sail. Look to the air, and there man's life is like a flying eagle. -- We are hastening to the grave. When our years do increase, our life doth decrease. -- Death creeps upon us by degrees. When our sight grows dim, there death creeps in at the eye. When our hearing is bad, death creeps in at the ear. When our legs tremble under us, death is pulling down the main pillars of the house: but *eternal life* comforts us against the shortness of natural life. That life to come is subject to no infirmities; it knows no period. We shall be *as the angels of God*, capable of no mutation or change. Thus you have seen six noble subjects for your thoughts to expatiate upon.

But where is the meditating Christian? -- Here I might lament the lack of holy meditation. Most people live in a hurry; they are so distracted with the cares of the world, that they can find no time to meditate or scarcely ask their souls how they do. We are not like the saints in former ages. David meditated in God's precepts, Psalm cxix. 15. 'Isaac walked in the evening to meditate,' Gen. xxiv. 63. He did take a turn with God. What devout meditations do we read in St. Austine and Anselm? But it is too much out of date among our modern *Terras Astraea reliquit.*

Those beasts under the law which did not chew the cud, were unclean. Such as do not chew the cud by holy meditation are to be reckoned among the unclean. But I shall rather turn my *lamentation* into a *persuasion*, entreating Christians to offer violence to themselves in this necessary duty of meditation. Pythagoras sequestered himself from all society, and lived in a cave for a whole year, that he might meditate upon philosophy. How then should we retire and lock up ourselves at least once a day, that we may meditate upon glory.

1. Meditation makes the Word preached to profit; it works it upon the conscience. As the bee sucks the flower, so by meditation we suck out the sweetness of a truth. It is not the receiving of meat into the mouth, but the digesting of it which makes it nutritive. -- So it is not the receiving of the most excellent truths in at the ear, that nourisheth our souls, but the digesting of them by meditation. -- Wine poured in a sieve, runs out. Many truths are lost, because Ministers pour their wine into sieves, either into leaking memories or feathery minds. Meditation is like a soaking rain, that goes to the root of the tree, and makes it bring forth fruit.

2. Holy meditation quickens the affections, Psalm cxix. 97. 'O how love I thy law! it is my meditation all the day.' The reason our affections are so cold to heavenly things is because we do not warm them at the fire of holy meditation. As the musing on amorous objects makes the fire of lust burn; the musing on injuries makes the fire of revenge burn: so meditating on the transcendent beauties of Christ, would make our love to Christ flame forth.

3. Meditation has a transforming power in it. The hearing of the Word may affect us;, but the meditating upon it doth transform us. Meditation stamps the impression of divine truths upon our hearts. By meditating on God's holiness, we grow holy. As Jacob's cattle, by looking on the rods, *conceived like the rods:* so while by meditation we look upon God's purity, we are changed into his likeness and are made partakers of his divine nature.

4. Meditation produceth reformation, Psalm cxix. 59. 'I thought on my ways, and turned my feet unto thy testimonies.' Did but people meditated on the damnableness of sin; did but they meddled with it,

there is a rope at the end of it, which will hang them eternally in hell, they would break off a course of sinning, and become new creatures. Let all this persuade us to holy meditation. I dare be bold to say that if men would spend but one quarter of an hour every day in contemplating heavenly objects, it would leave a mighty impression upon them, and, through the blessing of God might prove the beginning of a happy conversion.

But how shall we be able to meditate?

Get a love for spiritual things. We usually meditate on those things which we love. -- The voluptuous man can muse on his pleasures: the covetous man on his bags of gold. Did we love heavenly things, we would meditate more on them. Many say they cannot meditate, because they lack memory; but is it not rather because they want affection? Did they love the things of God, they would make them their continual study and meditation.

CPSIA information can be obtained
at www.ICGtesting.com
Printed in the USA
FSHW020006171120
75891FS

9 781599 255217